Live Life

FROM THE

Heart

52 Weeks to a Life of Passion and Purpose

Strategic Book Publishing and Rights Co.

The material in this publication is provided for informational purposes only. Procedures, laws and regulations are constantly changing and the examples given are intended to be general guidelines only. This book is sold with the understanding that no one involved in this publication is attempting herein to render professional advice.

Editor: Vern Westgate

Strategic Book Publishing & Rights Co. LLC
USA | Singapore
www.sbpra.net

Book Design: Linda W. Rigsbee

ISBN: 978-1-606935-51-4

*This book is dedicated to all those who are waiting for a
lifesaving transplant and to the memory of
those who died waiting.*

For information on how you can become an organ donor
go to: www.organ-donation-works.org
Make a decision. Share it with your family.
Someone's life could depend on it!

Acknowledgements

There are so many people to thank for their help in making this book a reality that I know I'll miss someone. To anyone who has touched my life in any way, I thank you for being the person you are.

To my parents who raised me to become the positive, driven person I am today: Without you I wouldn't be the person I am today. You've shown me what it means to be a contributing member of society. You laid the foundation to my self confidence to chase my dreams. Thank you.

To my wife Marise: You have been understanding and supportive through my journey of building a speaking career and writing this book. You made many sacrifices to help me make this happen. Thank You.

To the rest of my family, friends: grandparents, aunts and uncles and cousins, both those still with us and those no longer here, I thank you for enriching my life in many ways. You taught me what it means to love and be loved and for that I am forever grateful.

To Dawn McCabe and Trish Estabrooks who helped me clarify my thinking and molded my rants into a book that I hope others will read and understand. Thanks.

Finally, to you who bought this book. Thank you for investing in yourself. I hope this book provides you with insights and ideas that improve your life.

Contents

INTRODUCTION 1

USE YOUR LIFE

1. What If You Only Had a Year to Live? 11
2. You Are Here For a Reason 15
3. Live Today 19
4. Be Fully Present in Your Life 25
5. Strive to Live Without Regrets.............................29
6. Love With All of Your Heart...............................33
7. Don't Miss a Chance To Make a Difference 37
8. Create a Great Obituary 43
9. Be Your Own Hero..45
10. Be the Change...49
11. Give Your Time to Something That Will Outlast You........53

ATTITUDE

12. Look at Life With a Positive Perspective 59
13. Every Obstacle Is an Opportunity in Disguise 65
14. Adopt an Attitude of Gratitude 69
15. Cherish Your Struggles....................................73
16. Empathize Rather Than Criticize.........................77
17. When Criticism Is Necessary 79

GOALS

18. Awaken Your Potential 85
19. If You Believe It, You Can Achieve It 89
20. There Is Great Power in Beginning.......................93
21. Accept Nothing But the Best 97
22. Anything Is Possible...Really.............................101
23. Go Big or Stay Home 107
24. Make a Decision & Commit to it..........................111

25. Be Content But Never Be Satisfied.................................115
26. Fear Is For Failures 119

HABITS

27. You Are Your Habits..125
28. Work Hard...131
29. Read 135
30. Pray 139
31. Work Up a Sweat 143
32. Sing and Dance...147
33. Learn as Much as You Can 149
34. Watch What You're Watching 153
35. Get the Worm; Reach Your Goals 157
36. Get Some Sleep...161
37. You Can Always Sleep Tomorrow...................................165
38. Just Say No 167
39. Get More Done, Go to the Beach...................................171
40. Say Please and Thank You..175

FOCUS ON WHAT MATTERS

41. Focus...181
42. Make Time for What Counts to You..............................187
43. Beware the Lure of Money...191
44. Talk to Your Family...195
45. Keep in Touch..199
46. Don't Let Apathy Take Over 203
47. Take Care of # 1..207
48. Give as Much and as Often as You Can 211
49. The Give/Get Multiplication Principal..........................215
50. Make an Impact 219
51. Great Things Happen a Little at a Time 223
52. Refuse to Quit..227

"And in the end, it's not the years in your life that count. It's the life in your years." – **Abraham Lincoln**

Introduction

I want to start by thanking you for taking the time to read this book. I firmly believe that you've just made a great investment in your future and the quality of your life. I hope you enjoy reading this as much as I enjoyed writing it.

This book is a collection of lessons I learned over a period of twenty-two years battling a fatal illness and the six months that followed spent lying in a hospital bed praying for a miracle to save my life.

Those days were incredibly trying but they were also a great gift. During those six months, as I struggled to live, I learned valuable lessons about myself and my life. Those are the lessons that you will read in this book.

Since those days, I've been blessed with great health and have made a full recovery. I've spent the last five years living each day to the fullest and reflecting on my journey. My goal is to learn what I could and share the things I learned with you. I hope that in the following pages you will find messages that speak to your heart and that will be of practical value to you in your life.

Before I go further, I need to write a few words about why I wrote this book. How do I feel qualified to give advice. After all, I'm not a spiritual guru. I haven't started a successful corporation and I don't have a doctorate in psychology. However, I do have valuable information to share with you.

I consider the wisdom in this book to be incredibly valuable. This type of wisdom only comes from experiencing an incredible, life-altering, journey like the one that nearly took my life. That journey that taught me lessons about life that changed who I am. Here is the short version…

The Mark Black Story

In May 2001, after battling congenital heart disease since birth and at just twenty-three years of age, my doctor sat me down and broke the news that would change my life forever.

He explained that there was a potentially fatal complication to my already dangerous heart condition and unless I received a dangerous and rare heart and double-lung transplant, I wouldn't live to see my twenty-fifth birthday.

It was surreal sitting across from this man who had cared for me for years as he told me in no uncertain terms that my life was in danger. He explained that the surgery was incredibly risky. The five-year survival rate was only 50%. But without a new heart and new lungs, my chances of surviving for more than a year or two were slim. After consulting with my parents and other people I cared for and trusted I decided to take the risk.

The delicate procedure is performed in only three medical centers in Canada. Because donated lungs survive about six hours outside the body of a donor, I had to move within a two hour drive of the hospital where the surgery would take place.

My parents and I examined the available locations and decided on Toronto. We decided on Toronto for two reasons. First, we had family there. Knowing that I could wait two years or longer for a suitable donor, I wanted to be in a place where I had as much support as possible.

The second reason, and maybe the most important one, was that the transplant team at Toronto General Hospital had been doing lung transplants longer than any centre in the world. Heart and double-lung transplants are extremely rare. There hadn't been a single one done in the country in 2001. It was important to me to find the most experienced people.

In October, after being accepted on the transplant waiting list, my father and I left my Mom and three younger brothers at home in New Brunswick and moved the twelve hundred kilometers from home to start waiting.

When we arrived, the transplant coordinator gave me a pager. She told me to go to where I'd be staying in Toronto and wait for the pager to go off. When it rang, it would be the sign that a suitable donor had been found and I would come in to the hospital and have my transplant. It sounded so easy.

For four months I waited anxiously for the pager to go off. Every time the microwave beeped or the phone rang I jumped wondering if it was "the call." But months passed and the call didn't come.

We spent Christmas in Toronto, away from family and friends, because I couldn't leave and risk the possibility of missing my only chance at finding a suitable donor.

In April, after waiting for almost five months, I was admitted to the hospital for what was supposed to be "a few days" for some testing. Those "few days" became a week and then two, then a month. Finally I asked my doctor what was happening. She told me that my heart was getting worse.

I'd developed a condition called ventricular tachycardia. This meant that the bottom chambers of my heart, the ventricles, were spontaneously racing out of control. Every so often I would feel a pounding in my chest without warning. I knew that wasn't normal and that something was wrong. But there was nothing I could do to stop it.

My doctor explained that this new development meant I was at high risk for sudden cardiac arrest. At any moment, my heart could suddenly start racing and then stop without warning. If that happened and I didn't get immediate medical attention immediately I would die.

I was told that the only way to ensure my safety and prolong my life was to keep me in the hospital under 24-hour surveillance on a heart monitor. That way, if my heart rhythm didn't regulate on its own, they could intervene, administer a shock using a defibrillator and hopefully my heart would right itself.

I asked my doctor how long I would have to stay in the hospital. "Until you get a transplant", she answered. What she didn't say, but we both knew, was that with my heart deteriorating as badly as it was, the odds were good that I would be dead before that day came. So I made myself at home on the ninth floor of the Toronto General Hospital. I brought in my bedspread, clothes, posters and cards and turned that hospital room into home.

Those difficult days would prove to be one of my life's greatest blessings. With the realization that my life might end at any moment, I began to see my life in a new way. Suddenly, much of what I used to think was so important didn't matter.

Six months in hospital gave me the opportunity to spend time thinking about the things I'd always planned to do that I hadn't gotten around to yet. The things that I'd put off to do "someday". Now I realized that "someday" may never come.

During that time I promised myself that if I ever left the hospital, I wouldn't waste another day not pursuing my passions. I wouldn't let another day go by without living every moment to the fullest. I was going to start living life focused on the things that really mattered.

Finally, after ten months on the waiting list, one evening my nurse appeared at my door and said, "There is a call for you at the nurse's station". This was exciting news because I never got calls at the nurse's station.

As I walked down the hall, I wondered if perhaps this was the phone call I'd been waiting to get for almost a year. I picked up the phone and said, "Hello". The nurse on the other end of the line said the words that changed my life forever, "Mr. Black, I think we have a set of heart and lungs for you."

After a long pause while I tried to muster the appropriate words. I finally managed a "Thank You". The nurse on the phone explained that she would call again in a few hours to confirm that everything was a go.

I went back to my room feeling excited and nervous. I called my mom where she was staying in Toronto to let her know that she would have to come to the hospital. Then I called my family and friends back home in New Brunswick to tell them what was happening. While talking to them, I realized that they all sounded more nervous than I felt. Dorothy Bernard once said, "Courage is fear that has said its prayers." I was ready.

Finally, at about five in the morning, the surgeons came to get me for the surgery. There wasn't time for my mom and me to say everything we wanted to say to each other. I looked at my mom and she looked at me. Both of us were searching for the right words to say knowing that we might never see each other again. All I could think to say was, "Mom, I'll see you soon." I knew I had to be confident that everything would be okay.

I was in surgery for six or seven hours. Afterward the surgeons explained to my parents that things had gone as well as could be expected, but that I still had a long road of recovery ahead of me. I stayed in the intensive cardiac care unit for five days. Then I was transferred to the step-down unit and finally to the post-transplant floor.

I was fortunate to recover very quickly. Sixteen days after the surgery, I was discharged from the hospital. After living inside the same four walls for six months I was finally free! There was still a lot of work to do, but I'd been given a second chance. My life has just been changed in a significant and positive way.

The transformation continued after my transplant. I found myself looking at things differently. I had an increased sense of gratitude and a new appreciation for friends, family and time. I began to make decisions based on how much time I had to trade and if that sacrifice of time was worth it.

The experience totally changed my perspective on life. I became more focused on value rather than commodity; more concerned with quality than quantity; more focused on living in the moment than living for someday. It is from that new found perspective, that I've written this book.

This Book is For You

In the following pages you will find several ideas; some of them new, some not so new. Some you will agree with, some you won't. That's okay. Take what you can use and discard the rest. This book will speak in a different way to each person who reads. That's fine. In fact, that's my intention. There's something for everyone.

This book is intentionally divided into fifty-two chapters, one for each week of the year. I don't expect you to take a year to go through it although that would be great. I'm a realist. I realize that if you are attracted to a book like this one, you are likely already a driven and motivated person. You want to take action and you aren't going to take a year to read a book. That's okay.

Go ahead. Read the book cover to cover in one day if you like. In fact read it a few times and you'll see new things each time. But I also encourage you to keep it close and read one chapter a week. At the end of each chapter you'll find a section titled "In Black and White". You'll find a suggested action for you to take based on the concept discussed in that chapter. I encourage you to spend a week on each chapter. Complete as many of the suggested actions and incorporate as many of the concepts into your life as possible.

Don't just *read* this book but study it. Highlight it, underline it and write notes in the margins. Try the ideas suggested in the "In Black & White" section. My hope is that you will find ideas that you can implement immediately to improve your life in the fifty two chapters. They aren't deeply philosophical. In fact, I tried to make them exactly the opposite. They are intended to be very practical and easily applied. I want you to be able to put these things to use right away.

I believe that if you take just a handful of these ideas and put them into practice they will change your life. I wish you all the best in your journey and encourage you to always Live Life from the Heart!

Yours in the journey called life,

Mark Black

USE YOUR LIFE

"The whole life of man is but a point of time; let us enjoy it"
– Plutarch

CHAPTER 1

What If You Only Had A Year to Live?

I start many of my presentations with this question. I think it has powerful implications. Take a moment right now and seriously consider your answer to this question.

The simple act of asking yourself this question every so often can have a powerful focusing effect on your life. When we consciously think about how short life is we get serious about using the time that we have. At least that's what happened to me.

Before my transplant I was a twenty-three year old kid going to university with my whole life in front of me. My focus was mostly on myself and having fun. I wasn't concerned with spending time with my family or being right with myself and with my God. There would be time for that later I thought. I was wrong.

In the span of a few months during the summer of 2001, my life was turned upside down. I landed a great summer job as a tour guide on Parliament Hill in Ottawa and I had three days between the end of exams at university and the first day of training in Ottawa.

I came home to pack my bags, say goodbye to my family and head off for a great summer adventure. Instead, that day began a two-year saga that would change my life forever.

When I got home to pack my bags, my mom answered the door. She took one look at me and the colour left her face.

She immediately saw what I was denying. I'd lost more than thirty pounds. I was frail and sick. We would soon find out why. And we'd find that weight loss was the least of my problems.

My parents wasted no time taking me to see our doctor. Our family doctor immediately recognized that my condition was serious. He put me in hospital for monitoring while making arrangements to get me into a Halifax hospital to see the heart transplant team.

The cardiologist examined me that day and found I was in right and left-sided heart failure. My heart muscle was becoming thick, stiff and increasingly unable to fill with blood.

As the condition worsened my failing heart would cause my body to hold excess fluid and the fluid would accumulate throughout my body. First my hands and feet would swell painfully. Then in my lungs would fill making it very difficult to breathe.

When my condition grew severe, I struggled to climb a single flight of stairs without getting out of breathe. I would come home at the end of a morning of class and be totally exhausted. I needed a few hours on the couch just to find the energy to make supper.

DON'T LIVE EVERY DAY
LIKE IT'S YOUR LAST DAY
JUST LIVE EVERY DAY

When I saw my doctor that day, it didn't take him long to decide what had to happen. He reviewed some test results, looked at me and said the words that changed my life, "You need a heart and double lung transplant and you need it now."

Now it's five years later and odds are good that I will live much longer than a year. But I still ask myself often, "What if you only had a year to live?" Asking this question forces me to evaluate my priorities, remember that life is short and that I don't want to waste a single minute. I work hard to make sure that I am fully aware, alert and alive every minute of every day.

Many of us walk around 'existing' without really being alive. If you think about living like you only have a year to live, you'll gain sense of urgency about reaching your goals without a sense of panic.

Many people who have faced death will tell you that you to "Live every day like it's your last day!" I don't want you to do that. Imagine how exhausting it would be to try cramming a lifetime into twenty-hour hours.

Don't live every day like it's your last day. Just be ALIVE every day.

In Black & White

Spend this week thinking about what you really want to accomplish in your life. To help you along, answer these questions:

What would you do if you had a year to live?

What would be important? What wouldn't matter?

Do you want to DO more?

What would you do more?

What would you do less?

How would you use your time?

Once you have answers to these questions, write them down and put them where you will look at them every day. They'll help you to stay on track and remember what really matters.

"The mystery of human existence lies not in just staying alive, but in finding something to live for." – Fyodor Dostoyevsky

CHAPTER 2

You Are Here for a Reason

You are unique. In the 13 billion-year-history of the universe you are the only you that has ever been or ever will be. You are the only person to ever exist with your unique set of talents and abilities, your background and your passions. How powerful is that? What a gift… and what a responsibility!

I went through a severe depression after my transplant. After the initial high that comes from being given a second chance at life I crashed; hard.

It was hard to get out of bed in the morning. I struggled with dark thoughts, feelings of helplessness and hopelessness. For the first time in my life, thoughts of suicide crept into my mind. Although I was alive, I didn't know why. Why was I spared when others died? What was I supposed to do now? I struggled desperately to find a sense of purpose and meaning without success.

Call it survivor's guilt, or post-traumatic stress disorder, I couldn't find a compelling reason why I survived when so many others waiting for a transplant hadn't. The lack of a "why" ate at me every day.

After praying extensively, reading self-help books and the Bible and talking with family and friends, I found my answer: "I was made for a purpose." I may never fully realize it or even figure it out but I realize I *am* here for a reason. Even more importantly, I am the *only* me that has ever or will ever be who can fulfill that specific purpose.

No one who lived before me or will live after I'm gone will be exactly like me or will be better equipped to achieve what I have been uniquely created to do. The same is true for you!

You are truly unique. No matter how much you have in common with someone or how similar you are to your siblings, there is no one quite like you. You were born where you were, when you were, to the parents you were, with the gifts and talents you were, so you could accomplish what you are here to do.

DON'T SET OUT TO BE
THE NEXT SO-AND-SO;
BE THE ONLY YOU

In my chosen career it is very easy to watch colleagues and be envious. There is always someone who is doing something better, something hipper or something more unique than me. It is very tempting to find someone whom you admire and try to emulate them. In fact that was my strategy when I began my motivational speaking career. I thought that the best way for me to get better was to find those who were the best and copy them. Then I read something that changed my way of thinking not just about my career but about life. Don't set out to be the next so-and-so. Be the one and only you!

Are you always being compared to your parents or your siblings? Do you have a mentor or idol whom you greatly admire? That's fine, but don't let admiration become imitation. Oprah once said the greatest compliment anyone ever paid her was that she'd become more like herself. What a great thought and a great goal for your life! Strive to become more like you every day. You'll be giving yourself and the world the greatest gift you can give - you.

In Black & White

Take some silent time to consider why you are here? I know this is a daunting question. It is one you may never find a satisfactory answer to but that's okay. The pursuit for answers is still valuable. Think about your skills, talents and abilities. What are you uniquely equipped to do? Who are you meant to help?

"When I look back on all these worries, I remember the
story of the old man who said on his deathbed that he
had a lot of trouble in life, most of which never happened."
– Winston Churchill

CHAPTER 3

Live Today

This is an essential element to the philosophy I share with audiences. I realize it might not make immediate sense to some people. Live today? What does that mean? What other day is there to live but today?

Live today means exactly what it says: Live today. Live in the moment. Don't focus on tomorrow or yesterday, live today. You can put an end to worry and regret by learning how to live today. Worrying about tomorrow and regretting yesterday's mistakes stop you from living today.

During the course of my illness while listed for a transplant, the doctors decided to put me in the hospital for what was supposed to be a few days. I lost patience after two weeks and asked how long I would have to stay. My doctor told me I had developed ventricular tachycardia, a condition wherein the bottom chambers of the heart (the ventricles) randomly raced out of control.

Having this condition meant that I was at significant risk for going into cardiac arrest. Translation: I could die at any moment.

⋙

DON'T LIVE EVERY DAY
LIKE IT'S YOUR LAST,
JUST *LIVE* EVERY DAY

Learning that I could die at any moment was hard to hear. Living with that knowledge was even harder. I became paranoid and constantly worried that today was going to be the last day of my life. I'd go to sleep at night praying to God that I'd wake up in the morning and get to live another day. It was an incredibly stressful period in my life and I took it out on my parents. I was rude, I complained, I whined often that life was unfair.

After weeks of having to endure listening to me complain, my Mom had enough. She sat me down and shared this powerful wisdom.She said, "Mark, I know this isn't fair but the truth is there is nothing you can do about what's going on with your heart. If something is going to happen it's going to happen and there is nothing you can do about it. So you can worry if you want but all the worrying in the world isn't going to change things."

It took little while to appreciate what Mom was trying to tell me. Eventually I realized that she was telling me to live today. Fully experience and appreciate today. Let tomorrow take care of itself. This lesson helped me cope in those stressful times before my transplant and continues to help me today.

Although I've been fortunate to get second chance at life I still live with many things that I could worry about. I take more than a twenty pills every day just to survive.

Immune-suppressants, used to prevent rejection of my transplanted organs, leave me susceptible to infections and disease because my immune system is weakened. The side-effects of some of the medications include: increased risk of developing cancer, increased susceptibility to depression, kidney failure and liver disease.

The truth that I live with daily is that the very thing that saved my life will most likely be the cause of my death. Transplanted organs, especially lungs, are always subject to rejection and organ failure. Eventually, my new organs will stop working and I'll either be back on the transplant waiting list or, more likely, I'll die.

I could choose to spend each day worrying about what might happen to me. I could contemplate when the day will come that my organs stop working but I learned in that hospital room five years ago that all the worrying in the world does not change the situation. What I choose to do is live today as well as I can and let tomorrow take care of itself.

Many people who have faced life and death circumstances tell you that you should live every day like it's your last; please don't do that. Think about it for a moment. What would the world be like if everyone lived every day like it was their last day? Many would drive 200 km/hr and the sky would be full of skydivers! Don't live everyday like it's your last day, just *live* every day. Work hard to be fully *alive* every day of your life.

There are a lot of people in the world who are stuck living in the past. They spend their time reliving the good old days instead of making new good days.

Then there are people waiting for tomorrow to start living their lives. They're waiting for tomorrow to be happy and waiting for tomorrow to apologize for their mistakes and to tell someone that they love them. You may know someone like this. Perhaps you are a person like this. People who live for tomorrow are easy to spot. Because they use phrases like, "Someday, when I retire I'll…" "Someday when the kids move out I'll…" "Someday when I've saved up enough money I'll…" The problem with this approach to life is that far too often, "someday" never comes.

Tomorrow isn't promised to any of us. I don't say this to sound negative or make you worry but to help you realize that we all eventually run out of tomorrows. That's why it is so important to live today.

Life is too short to be live as a goal-oriented event or check list of to dos and appointments. If your attitude is that the destination is all that matters, you'll end up disappointed. It's not all about where you get or what you get, how you get there also matters.

In Black & White

Resist the temptation to worry about tomorrow. Realize that no matter how badly you regret yesterday nothing you can do will change it now. This week, make a concerted effort to stay focused on the moment.

Don't preoccupy yourself by what is coming up in ten minutes or ten weeks. And don't waste time re-living past mistakes. Live today as best as you can and let tomorrow take care of itself.

TRY THE ELASTIC EXERCISE:

Put an elastic band around your wrist (use a thick rubber band that won't break). Wear the rubber band for a whole week. Whenever you feel your consciousness drifting towards the past or future, switch the elastic to your opposite wrist. Or to really make a point, snap the elastic each time. This exercise will help you recognize when your focus drifts.

When that happens, stop and be in the present. Take a deep breath and revel in being alive. When you learn to live today well and appreciate the present, I promise that the rest will take care of you.

"Know the true value of time; snatch, seize and enjoy every moment of it. No idleness; no laziness; no procrastination; never put off tomorrow what you can do today"
– Lord Chesterfield

CHAPTER 4

Be Fully Present in Your Life

I missed yesterday. Most of it anyway. I let it slip right by. I wasted the whole day by focusing on what would happen later in the week. I waited for the day to end so I could wake up and start working on tomorrow. As a rule I don't do that, but yesterday I failed. That's okay. We all fail sometimes but tomorrow I'll work hard to be present.

**TO STAY PRESENT IN
YOUR LIFE MEANS BEING
FULLY ALIVE AND AWARE
EVERY MOMENT
OF EVERY DAY**

What's wrong with thinking about the future? There's nothing wrong with thinking ahead. The problem arises when you fixate on tomorrow at the expense of today. Our inability to live in the present causes many people to live unhappy, unfulfilled lives. Many are busy planning the next thing in their lives or re-living past mistakes so they fail to be fully present in the only time that they can do anything about, today.

Have you ever had a conversation with someone whose mind was somewhere else? Isn't it frustrating? More importantly, the person you were talking to, or at least trying to talk to, missed a conversation. They missed time they will never experience again.

Staying present in your life means being fully alive and aware every moment of every day. It's a challenge. Especially considering how we live our lives. To be truly present we have to resist the temptation to be pulled in one direction or another by the multitude of distractions around us. You have to be able to stay 100% in THIS moment.

What are you thinking about right now? If you have more than one answer or your answer isn't "staying present in my life", you can see how hard the quest to live in the present can be.

We live in a fast-paced, grab-it-and-go world. The society we live in rewards, even reveres, those who are NEVER EVER PRESENT! Those multi-taskers who talk on the phone, while eating dinner, while doing laundry and paying bills. We are considered superior if we sit in a meeting, send email on our Blackberry and plan our weekend at the same time.

What's the problem with that? Nothing, if your focus is quantity. But life is about more than the *quantity* of things we accomplish. Isn't it about the *quality* of the experience? If it's about the *quality* of the experience, why are we in such a hurry to get done?

Don't misunderstand. We are all incredibly busy. Chances are good that life would be very difficult to manage if we never did more than one thing at a time. We have dozens of activities to complete in a day's run that require minimal attention. But I think in our endless pursuit of efficiency we lose sight of why we multi-task in the first place.

Didn't we invent dishwashers, computers, cell phones and microwaves, so we could be more efficient and have more time for what really matters? Then are so many of us glued to our computer screens instead of talking with real people? Why do many families only eat dinner together on holidays?

In Black & White

Here some ideas to help you stay present:

1. **Revel in Meal Preparation** – What if you turned everything off except some mood music, and enjoyed, even reveled, in cooking a good meal tonight? You did this instead of watching the news, tidying the house, and doing laundry while you cook.

What if you were present while you chopped carrots and peeled potatoes? What if you paused to enjoy the sensory experience of cooking; the sound of boiling water, the smell of garlic sautéing in a pan, the brilliant colours of red peppers and spinach?

Many people, I among them, find cooking to be a relaxing, even therapeutic, experience. However, it loses its charm when I do five other things at the same time.

2. If cooking isn't your thing, try being fully present doing something else. Have a phone conversation without watching television or surfing the net at the same time. Just listen and talk. Or try going for a walk or a run and only focus on your breathing

3. If you're a parent I suggest that you set aside a half-hour each night to sit down and eat dinner as a family. Make supper time, sacred time, not to be interrupted by anything.

"Someone once said that a family that prays together stays together." I believe that a family that eats together stays together (it doesn't rhyme, but it's just as true). Eat, talk, and enjoy each other's company rather than letting business, television, or the phone get in the way.

There are too few hours in a day for us to devote 100% of our energy and attention to menial tasks and there's no need to do that. Take time this week to find at least one activity that you can do with all of your attention. When the week is over, evaluate how it made you feel.

You'll discover that when you give a worthy thing 100% of your attention, and you are fully present, you get more enjoyment from what you are doing. More importantly, being fully alive each day brings a sense of peace and contentment that few things can.

Set aside a few minutes a day to ponder these questions. You'll eventually receive the message you need to hear. I can't promise you'll find the whole answer, I'm not sure I have. But you'll find what you need.

"Nowadays most people die of a sort of creeping common sense, and discover, when it is too late, that the only things one never regrets are one's mistakes."
– Oscar Wilde

CHAPTER 5

Strive to Live Without Regrets

One of my goals in life is to get to the end of it, look back at how I've used my time and be able to say without reservation that I did my best. I want to be able to say that I used my time well and did the best that I could with what I had. No regrets. No person that I should have loved better, no opportunity that came my way that I didn't take advantage of, no chance that I should have taken but didn't.

Let me be clear about what I mean by regrets. I don't mean to suggest that I expect to get through my life without making any mistakes; I don't think that's possible. In fact, if you get through life without making mistakes, either you aren't being honest with yourself or haven't really lived.

Are there people in your life that you've grown apart from that you wish you were closer to? Are you holding a grudge against a family member or friend? Have you given up on a dream because you've lost the motivation? Now is the time to do something.

Life is finite. It WILL end. And when it does, it will be too late to try that new thing, forgive that old friend or pursue that big goal. I say that not to scare you but to motivate you to take action, today.

If I learned anything from my battle with congenital heart disease, a transplant, and facing my own death, it's that life is too short to wait for anything. Tomorrow isn't promised to any of us, so take advantage of today.

Make yourself a life-long to-do list. Think of all of the things that you'd like to experience and accomplish. Write them down and start working and crossing them off.

**NOW IS THE TIME TO DO
SOMETHING. LIFE IS
FINITE; IT WILL END. AND
WHEN IT DOES, IT WILL
BE TOO LATE TO TRY
THAT NEW THING,
FORGIVE THAT OLD
FRIEND, OR PURSUE
THAT BIG GOAL**

If you get through your life and cross everything off of your "To Do List" I have two things to say to you: "Congratulations on a great accomplishment", AND "Why haven't you added more things to the list?"

Life is short. Even if you live to be 110 there will never be enough time to experience everything worth experiencing, meet everyone worth meeting, listen to every great piece of music, read every great book or visit every fun place.

Does that mean that you can't be happy and fulfilled unless you've seen and experienced a certain number of things? Do you need to cross off a certain number of items to consider your life well-lived? I don't think so.

To me, a life well-lived depends much more on how you lived your life than on what you spent your time doing. In other words, it isn't where you've been or what you've done that matters. Happiness can't be correlated to an arbitrary number of experiences. The real key is to be satisfied with what you've been able to see and experience while continually striving to experience and learn more.

There will always be something else to do, or somewhere else to visit, and while I don't think we should be too focused on doing, I also think we have to be careful not to fall into the we've "Been there, done that" thinking trap.

In Black & White

First, if you don't have a Life's To Do List, make one right now. Here is mine:

- Visit Europe, South America, Africa and Asia
- Publish my biography
- Read the Bible
- Run 10 marathons
- Pray Everyday
- Run a sub 4:00 marathon

- **Be Romantic Every Week**
- **Make $200,000 a year as a Speaker**
- **Create a foundation for people waiting for transplants**

This is by no means an exhaustive list. I plan to add more to it as I cross things off it.

Creating a list is powerful for two reasons:

- One, it helps you discover what it is that you really want from your life and,

- Two; it keeps you focused on those goals so that you work continuously to achieve them.

Take time this week and make your list. Print it and post it where you'll see it often. Crossing things off of that list is empowering. It will give you a glimpse at just how much power you have in shaping your own destiny. Remember, the only one who has to live your life is you. So make sure you're living your life in a way that makes you feel satisfied and proud.

"All you need is love" – The Beatles

CHAPTER 6

Love
With All Your Heart

Love. As far as I'm concerned it's what life is all about. As the Beatles sang, "It's all you need." With love you feel like you can take on the world. Without it every challenge and obstacle you face looms larger than it should.

❧

**TO LIVE A FULFILLING,
JOYOUS, LIFE YOU MUST
LEARN TO LOVE WITH
ALL YOUR HEART**

Within you lies a deep-seated desire to love and to be loved. It's imprinted on your heart the moment you're born. In order to live a fulfilling, joyous life you must learn to love with all your heart.

Many people go through life missing out on this most beautiful of life's gifts. You probably know someone who lives a virtually loveless life. It can happen for all kinds of reasons: a broken heart, a failed relationship, abuse or any number of other reasons.

More often than not, a person who lives without love in their lives does so because love let them down at some point. Love failed them and they were hurt so badly they avoid the possibility of love for fear of experiencing that pain again.

Do you know someone like that? Are you someone like that?

When I was 20 years old, in my second year of university, I fell in love. I had it bad. We were best friends and we got along great. She was beautiful. I loved her and she loved me. We had tough times like everyone does, but we always recovered. Then I got sick.

I had to move to Toronto to wait for my transplant, but my girlfriend, based in New Brunswick at the time, had to continue her studies. She couldn't afford to drop everything and come to be by my side.

We continued a long distance relationship for several months, talking on the phone and sending emails back and forth. But slowly, the distance and the circumstances took a toll on our relationship.

Looking back I can see what incredibly different places we were in. We were both in our early twenties. She was planning her future and planting the seeds for the rest of her life. I was just a year younger and facing the possibility that my life might soon be over. After weeks of agonizing telephone conversations she did the best thing she could do for me. She broke up with me.

I was crushed. From what I could see, she was the person I was supposed to spend the rest of my life with. We were meant to be together. After my transplant, I thought we'd get married, have children and live happily ever after. She knew that would never work.

For weeks after she told me it was over I continued talking with her. Each time I tried to make her see how we were perfect for each other and that we just had to make it over this hurdle. Thankfully she knew better. She realized that God had another plan for each of us and had the courage to make the right decision.

Those days are long past now and I have a wonderful life with my wife and kids. But I never would have had this new life if I had allowed my past to control my future. I often wonder where I would be if I'd allowed that past hurt to stop me from loving again. How much would I have missed out on? How much joy would I never have experienced?

In Black & White

If you're single or married, young or old you deserve to have love in your life. If you haven't found the love you're looking for yet, don't panic. Keep putting love into the world and I promise it will come back to you.

This week, list five things that may be preventing love from coming into your life. Once you've identified these barriers, work at trying to remove them.

How am I Preventing Love from Coming in to My Life?

_____

_____

_____

*"I expect to pass through this life but once. If, therefore,
there can be any kindness I can show, or any good thing
I can do to any fellow being let me do it now, for
I shall not pass this way again." – **William Penn***

CHAPTER 7

Don't Miss a Chance to Make a Difference

Life is short. Just ask me. I've lived with a constant reminder of the fragility of life from the day I took my first breath. After coming close to death and enduring a risky and dangerous surgery, the value of each day is apparent and you realize that tomorrow isn't guaranteed. The fact is, while some of us live with greater risks than others, tomorrow isn't promised to anyone. Life is fragile.

Does that mean you should live in fear of the potential problems you might have to face? Of course not. Many people live with paralyzing fear every day. They will be the first to say that it can make you crazy.

While we shouldn't live in constant worry, we do need to remember how short and precious our time is and let that serve to motivate us to let no opportunity pass us by. As William Penn said, "I shall not pass this way again."

If we're lucky in life opportunity will knock once in a while. However, the times when it will knock twice are very rare.

So I urge you not to let a single opportunity pass you by and pay special attention to those opportunities to "do any good thing for our fellow man."

If I sum up the primary goal for my life in one sentence, it would be this, "To leave the world a little bit better for my having lived in it." That's it. I have many other ambitions and goals, but they all point at helping me achieve that one thing.

I believe it takes all of us working together, each fulfilling his or her purpose, to make the world better. Whether that comes in the form of providing for your family as a parent, teaching and inspiring young people to do great things as a teacher, protecting and maintaining the peace as a police officer or providing a clean and healthy environment as a janitor, we all share the responsibility to play a part in making the world a better place.

Assuming that you would like to make the world a better place, why are you guilty of allowing opportunities to make a difference slip through your fingers?

"Now wait a minute" you say, "You don't know me Mark. How do you know what I'm doing with my life? How do you know if I'm letting opportunities pass me by?"

You're right. I don't know you, yet I'll bet that you missed an opportunity to make a difference yesterday. Take this quiz to see how often you let opportunities to make a difference pass you by.

Answer the following questions on a scale from 1 to 10 where 1= never and 10 = always and be the judge.

How often have I:

- Failed to let someone out at an intersection?
- Failed to hold a door for someone because they were just a bit too far away?
- Walked past a piece of garbage without picking up?
- Walked past a pan handler because, "If he needs money he should get a job like the rest of us."
- Told a racist, sexist or derogatory joke?
- Laughed at one of those jokes?
- Did the easy thing instead of what I knew was right?
- Supported the work of a musician, artist or actor whose work was racist, violent, or sexist?
- Told a lie, allowed someone to tell a lie for me or simply failed to tell the truth, because it was easier than being completely honest?
- Been moved to anger by the injustice suffered by my fellow human beings and did nothing about it?

Total: _____

I challenge anyone to score a 10 on that test. I think if your score is under 25 you're doing really well.

No matter what your score, the point to that little quiz is that it can help you identify ways in which you might take advantage of more opportunities. I've certainly been guilty of failing to do each of these things throughout life. But asking myself these questions and being aware of my behavior is the first step toward improving.

You may feel like these behaviours are insignificant or that we all fail so who cares? What kind of difference will my effort to stop doing any these things make in the world?

Honestly, if you are the only one to change, probably not much. But you're doing these little things on a consistent basis influences people with whom you are connected and they influence people they know, then it could make a big difference.

If you change the world of those connected to you by making their lives better, happier, safer and full of love, then you changed that person and their world. More importantly, you gave them the motive and drive to do the same for the people in their lives.

I believe one person can change the world. I believe one person can be a catalyst and their passion can spark a movement that can change the world.

One of my favorite examples is Craig Kielburger. You may recognize the name of this courageous young leader, but for those who don't, let me tell you a bit about him.

Craig Kielburger was watching the news when he was twelve years old. He heard the tragic story of a child laborer a world away who was murdered.

Craig could have done what most people did and changed the channel or listened with sympathy and forgot about it five minutes later. But twelve year old Craig Kielburger had the courage to try to change things.

This courageous twelve year old took action that many others dared not. He started a non-profit organization called Free the Children and harnessed the enthusiasm of young people. He fought for the rights of other children half-way across the world.

Free the Children has changed the lives of more than 1,000,000 young people around the world, built 450 schools and provides education to more than 40,000 children every day.

**I BELIEVE THAT ONE PERSON
CAN BE A CATALYST AND
THAT THEIR PASSION CAN SPARK A
MOVEMENT THAT CAN CHANGE
THE WORLD.**

All that good was done because a twelve year old boy from Ottawa saw injustice and decided not to look away.

You *can* change the world and you can do it by changing your world. If we all make the effort to change our world, and those we influence make the same effort and so on, we influence the lives of everyone on the planet. It will be a slow process but that doesn't make it any less powerful.

Let this be your life's mission: "Let no day go by where you don't touch the life of someone else in a positive way." If you do this, you'll have lived well.

In Black & White

Spend time this week searching your life for opportunities that you have overlooked that would allow you to make a difference. Select one of the missed opportunities you discovered in the quiz and make it a point never to miss it again.

Opportunities to Make a Difference That I've Missed:

_____

_____

_____

_____

What will I do differently next time?

_____

_____

_____

_____

"May you live all the days of your life."
– Jonathan Swift

CHAPTER 8

Create a Great Obituary

We've talked a little about goals but we haven't really addressed a question many of us have asked at some point in life, "How do I figure out what goals I should have in the first place?"

In a world with so many possibilities, sometimes our biggest challenge is trying to decide what we want from our lives. If you've ever sat down to write out your lifetime goals and had trouble deciding what to write try this: write your obituary.

**WRITE YOUR OBITUARY
THEN LIVE YOUR LIFE IN
A WAY THAT MAKES IT TRUE**

I got this idea when I read an obituary whose author and subject was the same person. She had written her own obituary. I don't suggest you do this unless you want to. To me it seemed weird, even creepy. But I think the idea has merit as a goal setting exercise.

In Black & White

The key to getting the most out of this exercise is to be sure that you don't limit yourself by only writing what you have or will soon accomplish. Write it as though its 50 years from now. Your life has gone exactly as you hoped it would and you've accomplished everything you wanted to.

This task shouldn't be done in ten minutes. I recommend that you live with the question for a day or two, before you start writing.

When you're ready write a first draft. Include everything you find in a regular obituary: surviving family members (even if they are only imagined at this point in your life), your job (the one you *want* to have), community involvement, accomplishments and anything else that you'd want people to be able to say about you.

When you finish writing, read it over and make any changes you want. Re-write as many times as necessary to make it just right. Once you're pleased with the result, print it out and post it where you will see it every day.

Now for the challenge—to make what you've written a reality.

"We all live in suspense from day to day; in other words, we are the hero of our own story"
– Mary McCarthy

CHAPTER 9

Be Your Own Hero

I've noticed lately that there seems to be a shortage of heroes in our world.

As a kid, I looked up to sports heroes. Athletes weren't just sports superstars, they were successes in life. They were people to admire and I looked up to them. Unfortunately, times have changed. Now instead of Michael Jordan, Cal Ripken Jr. and Wayne Gretzky we have OJ Simpson, Barry Bonds and Pete Rose.

Other people idolize musicians, but lately it seems social revolutionaries like John Lennon and Bob Dylan have been replaced by those with questionable talent, out to make money and live the fast life. People like Snoop Dog, Paris Hilton and 50 Cent, who've been in and out of jail and tabloids too often to count, are certainly not people any of us should model our lives after.

Then there are our "inspiring" politicians. The people who are in positions where public perception is most important and quality leadership is paramount have let us down for years. So when today's generation is looking for new heroes what are we to do?

YOUR SUCCESS IS NO
ONE'S RESPONSIBILITY
BUT YOURS

Am I saying that there is no one left to look up to? Of course not. Bono, David Suzuki, Oprah and the Dalai Lama are examples of well known people who do heroic things to improve our world and the lives of others. They should be admired and emulated but I don't necessarily think that they should be your heroes.

My hope is that our current lackluster roster of heroes will help us realize that we should not depend on celebrities, athletes or government officials to be our heroes.

It's great to have people who motivate and inspire us in our life. But in the end we're born and we die alone. Your success is no one's responsibility but yours.

In a world where kids are born with a sense of entitlement, taking responsibility for your success is a concept I think we desperately need to embrace.

I encourage you to start thinking about yourself as your own hero this week. Live life in a way that you inspire yourself. This may sound egotistical, but note I don't say *admire* yourself or look up to yourself, I said *inspire* yourself.

In Black & White

List of your proudest achievements and put it where you can refer to it often. Whenever you need a boost or need a reminder of what you're capable of, look at that list. Remind yourself that you did these things. You'll instantly feel more confident and capable.

The Achievements I'm Most Proud Of:

_____

_____

_____

_____

"We are so often left to wonder whether one person can possibly make a difference. Mother Teresa said yes we can. Her life was resounding proof that it is possible."
– Craig Kielburger

CHAPTER 10

Be the Change...

"Be the change you want to see in the world." Mahatma Gandhi once said about making the world a better place. What a powerful statement!

Most of us would have no trouble making a list of what's wrong with our world. It might not be an exhaustive list but it would certainly be long. If I asked you to grab pen and paper and list 25 things wrong with the world today you could do it in less than five minutes! (Go ahead, try it.)

The question is; if you're so good at identifying what's wrong why haven't you done anything about it? I apologize if that sounds accusatory—actually on second thought, I'm not sorry. It's supposed to be accusatory. I don't say that I do much more than anyone else, but we all need to look in the mirror and ask ourselves; what am I doing to make the world a better place?

Maybe you tell yourself the reason you haven't done anything is that it wouldn't make a difference; that the problems are so big and you're just one person. Or you may think, "I'd love to help, but I don't know where to start." Those are common, under - standable reactions but those aren't really answers, they're just excuses.

The truth is the reason our world is in the state it is with wars raging, our environment in crisis and thousands dying from curable illnesses on one continent while others live in luxury on another, is because far too many of us take the attitude that we can't make a difference.

If we all recognize the power we have to make a difference and take action, our world would be a better place.

WAR, FAMINE, INEQUALITY AND INJUSTICE DON'T EXIST AS MUCH BECAUSE OF WHAT THE 'BAD PEOPLE' IN THE WORLD ARE DOING, AS BECAUSE OF WHAT THE BILLIONS OF WELL-INTENTIONED PEOPLE *AREN'T* DOING

What do you want to change in the world around you? Decide and start taking action today. Do you feel like the world has become too cold and unfriendly? Then *do* something to warm it up and make it friendlier.

You could try Juan Mann's idea. Juan gained fleeting fame on You Tube by standing on the streets of downtown Chicago wearing a sign that read: Free Hugs" and spent days giving free hugs to anyone who would let him.

After several days giving out hugs to some and enduring rejection from many Juan generated such a buzz in the media that he was invited to be a guest on Oprah. His message of kindness was shared with millions of people around the world! He was one guy who made a big difference with a simple, yet powerful, act.

Will you take action that gets you on Oprah? Probably not. But it will make a difference. Show others that it's possible for one person to have an effect on the world and you'll motivate others to do the same.

War, famine, inequality and injustice don't exist as much because of what "bad people" in the world do as because of what billions of well-intentioned people *aren't* doing! So go out and do something, anything to make the world just a little bit better. You won't solve all the world's problems but you will make a difference.

In Black & White

Go back to your list of things that are wrong with the world. Prioritize the top five you feel most passionate about. If these problems are major issues that can't be solved overnight, that's okay. You can still make a difference.

Your next step is to think. You might have to do research and determine what your most effective action is.

I'm all for thinking big, but don't think so big that you won't be able to take action right away. That's the key. You MUST take action. The world changes more when millions take small actions than when one person takes a big action.

Don't fall into the trap of waiting until you win your billions or until the time is just right before you do something. Take action now!

Here are a few suggestions of things you can do today to start making a difference:

- Volunteer at your local hospital, soup kitchen, school or senior's centre.
- Be a big brother or big sister.
- Write a letter to your elected government representative about an important issue.
- Organize a food drive for the local food bank.
- Make a meal for someone.
- Volunteer with an NGO or charity.
- Sponsor a child in a foreign country.
- Spend time picking up trash in your neighbourhood or the highway.
- Help build a home with Habitat for Humanity.
- Join an organization like Free the Children.

Maybe you'll become so passionate about a cause that you single-handedly change the world. Even if you aren't, if you take action you *will* make a difference.

"The great use of life is to spend it for something that will outlast it." – **William James**

CHAPTER 11

Give Your Time to Something That Will Outlast You

No matter your age, gender, social status, ethnicity, nationality, religion or cultural background, we all share a few common desires: to belong, to love and be loved and to be immortal.

Maybe you don't want to live forever. I know I don't. Imagine how hard it would be to get out of bed at 216 years old. But we all do want to live on in some way. We want to leave a legacy. That's what this chapter is about. How can you live your life so that you leave behind something of value?

How do you build a great legacy? There are a few ways. Some live on in movies, songs, inventions and books. However, the best way to build a legacy is through giving. Winston Churchill once said, "We make living by what we get but we make a life by what we give." So what are you giving to the world?

For many, our biggest contribution to society will be raising happy, healthy and productive children. (If you don't think that's important, look what happens when parents fail to do that.)

~~~

WE MAKE A LIVING BY WHAT WE GET, BUT WE MAKE A *LIFE* BY WHAT WE *GIVE*

Your children and grandchildren will likely become your life's greatest legacy. That's why I believe it's so important for us to ensure that we spend time on things that will outlive us. Whether that means spending time with your kids, voluntee - ring for a charity or making improvements in your community, make sure you spend time building your legacy.

An old adage says no one lying on their deathbed ever wished they'd spent more time at the office. Most of us acknowledge the truth of that statement. But how many make practical decisions about how to live our lives that reflect our knowledge that work and money are not the most important things in life?

We all want to be remembered for the right reasons. That doesn't happen by accident. So take a moment to figure out what you want to be remembered for and what you will do to get it done.

In Black & White

Sometimes the hardest part of this lesson is knowing where to start. To help you, I've given you a few questions to help you discover what is truly important for you.

Complete the following sentences:

I want to be remembered as someone who;

_____

_____

To be remembered that way, I have to:

_____

_____

When I die, the thing that I want to leave behind is;

_____

_____

The most important thing in my life is

_____

_____

My definition of success is;

_____

_____

Now for the real challenge; you've established what you want to achieve and what really matters to you. Live your life accordingly.

ATTITUDE

*"The greatest discovery of my generation is that a human
being can alter his life by altering his attitudes of mind"*
– William James

CHAPTER 12

Look at Life With a Positive Perspective

I like to think that one of the major benefits of my inspirational programs is they give my audiences a healthy dose of perspective. Every time I take the stage I strive to help the people in my audiences see their lives from a different point of view; a more positive perspective.

A good sense of perspective can go a long way toward helping you be a more positive, productive and stress-free person. In fact changing your perspective can change your reality.

A sad truth in life is that many people never reach their full potential. I think it's due to a lack of perspective much of the time. It's easy to be so focused on our problems and challenges that we become overwhelmed and give up on trying to achieve our dreams out of frustration, lack of confidence, or fear of failure. I believe if those people had a better perspective they might see that the obstacles that stood in their way weren't insurmountable.

When I give keynote speeches and seminars, I suggest to my audience that what they might find a major obstacle in their life is not so serious when compared with what other people have dealt with and overcome.

∼≈≋⊘

BY CHANGING YOUR PERSPECTIVE, YOU CAN CHANGE YOUR REALITY

My perspective on life changed forever because of my transplant. After enduring six months in hospital and ten months of stress on the organ transplant wait list, waiting an extra day for a delivery wasn't so hard. Stare death in the face for months and getting stuck in traffic isn't a big deal. After enduring seven hours of surgery, having 30 staples and a half a dozen tubes in my chest, getting a cold isn't quite so annoying.

Does this mean that if you change your outlook and adopt a more positive perspective you won't have any more problems? Of course not.

Does it mean that since I've been through these things and adopted a positive perspective on life, I never get frustrated sitting in traffic? I wish I could say "yes" but the truth is that I still catch myself yelling at the guy in front of me who's had his turn signal on for three minutes!

However, while I slip up from time to time, I've adjusted my perspective and my outlook is different. I'm more patient, less stressed and handle challenges better. I still have work to do in these areas, but that's part of life isn't it?

I want to help you to adjust your perspective this week.

If you want to be more positive and want a more optimistic outlook on life, there are lots of things you can do. The question is; do you really want to change?

If you don't feel any need to change stop reading. The rest of this chapter won't help you. But if you want to be more positive and you'd like to see things in a brighter light, keep reading. These simple steps will help turn your attitude around.

In Black & White

1. Decide to Be Optimistic

This idea sounds simple because it is. But *knowing* something and *doing* it are two different things. The most important thing you can do to become more positive is to make the *decision* to be optimistic.

What does that mean? It means you don't wait to start feeling happier. You don't wait until your life conditions are such that you suddenly *become* more optimistic. You *decide* to be optimistic right now. You decide to react to problems as challenges rather than obstacles.

At first this takes work. Undoing bad habits is rarely easy. Over time however, being positive *will* become your new habit. You begin noticing you handle things with greater optimism and a more positive attitude.

2. Eat, Sleep, Run and be Merry

We often sabotage our efforts to be positive and happy before we even start. We swim upstream from the beginning. From a purely physiological perspective, our mood, attitude and thus our perspective on life comes down to firing neurons and secreting hormones.

While our mood is certainly not ruled entirely by body chemistry, if these things are out of whack, it can make the battle that much more difficult. The bad news is that you may be doing everything else right, but if you aren't doing the things I'm about to tell you, all your efforts may be for naught. The good news is that if that IS the case a few simple changes may make all the difference.

Sleep – Numerous studies conclude that the amount of sleep we get, or don't get, can dramatically affect our mood and outlook on life. If you aren't getting at least 7 1/2 hours of sleep every night, start tonight. Lack of sleep can cause fatigue, anxiety and depression. All these will severely inhibit your ability to hold a positive perspective on life.

Run – I already hear many of you gasping. If regular physical activity isn't a part of your schedule, you need to find time to fit it in. Walking from the couch to the fridge doesn't constitute physical activity. You need at least twenty minutes of vigorous activity 3-4 times a week to get the benefits. But wow is it worth it!

People who exercise regularly experience better and more stable moods, a feeling of control over their life, greater self-worth and a more positive attitude.

Eat – I know you're already doing this right? Okay, but HOW are you doing it? Eating right has a major impact on your personal effectiveness and your mental fitness.

With all of the different diets out there today, how do you know what's right? The truth is, while each diet may present certain benefits over others, the most effective and healthy diet is the one you've known about most of your life. It's called the four food groups!

Get a balanced mix of all the food groups, eat natural, whole foods, and drink plenty of water. That's all you need to do to benefit mentally from what you eat.

Are you *carb conscious*? If you are on a high protein/low carb diet craze be careful, especially at breakfast. Your brain needs fuel and carbohydrates are its number one source. Depriving yourself of all carbohydrates can make your brain sluggish. So by all means eat eggs and cheese and drink milk, just make sure that you also have juice and toast too. Your brain will thank you.

3. If All Else Fails, Fake It!

If this sounds like I'm asking you to lie, well I am—sort of, at least to yourself. If your attitude is negative it can be more difficult to make the attitudinal changes I talk about here.

If you having trouble initially feeling more positive or looking at things more optimistically, fake it.

Force a smile. Be polite when you don't feel like it. Force yourself to see a positive alternative to a situation even if you don't believe it. It will feel forced and unnatural at first. But practice makes perfect even when it comes to attitude.

Does this mean you need to be positive all of the time? Am I suggesting that you should suppress or ignore negative feelings? Absolutely not. Bad feelings are as critical to life as good ones. It's okay to feel bad, to feel down and to be depressed, sometimes. It's also important to know when it's time to try to snap yourself out of it.

The more you practice being a positive, optimistic person, the less you have to pretend. Before long you find that what used to be difficult has become natural. Is that hard to believe? Try it for two weeks and then let me know how it goes

"No pessimist ever discovered the secret of the stars, or sailed to uncharted land, or opened a new heaven." – Helen Keller

CHAPTER 13

Every Obstacle Is Just an Opportunity in Disguise

At twenty-two my life suddenly began to crumble around me. While attending university and working on an education degree, my heart condition suddenly grew worse. I got so sick that I lost thirty pounds and was hospitalized for more than six months. Finally, after waiting for nearly a year on the waiting list, I underwent a heart and double-lung transplant. It was truly a miracle. The transplant gave me a second chance at life and I was extremely grateful.

Unfortunately, while my life was saved, my career hopes were dashed. Doctors said that the immune-suppressant drugs I had to take every day to prevent rejection of my organs meant I would always be at a high risk of contracting infections and diseases. School was one of the worst places for me to be. Those of you with children know nobody carries germs like children. The doctors said I should find another line of work to protect my health and my transplant.

After dreaming of being a teacher most of my life, that door was slammed in my face. At that point in my life I was faced with a choice. I could choose to get upset, feel bad for myself and cry "poor me" for the next few years. Or I could choose to stay positive and decide that not being able to teach was God's way of telling me that I was meant to do something else.

❧

IF WE'RE READY TO LISTEN, THE OBSTACLES WE FACE CAN BE LIFE'S WAY OF PUSHING US IN THE RIGHT DIRECTION

A year after the door to teaching closed a window opened. I started doing presentations about the importance of organ donation to schools, companies and associations. I was happy to volunteer my time just to get the message out. (For information about how you can become an organ donor, go to: www.organ-donation-works.org.)

Over the next few months I came to realize that I loved speaking to people and sharing my message. From there I started to use my story to backdrop my motivational message to Live Life from the Heart. I soon had a full-time career as a speaker and consultant.

When the door on my teaching career closed, it could have been another crisis in my life. Fortunately for me I was positive, prepared and persistent. I recognized the opportunity to turn volunteer presentations into a career; I learned what I needed to learn and I was persistent enough to stick with it despite facing repeated rejection.

Life has a way of getting us down at times. When things get really rough it can feel like life has it in for us. But the truth is that there is no conspiracy against us and no one is out to get us. Life is just hard sometimes. That doesn't mean we have to suffer. What it means is that we have to be tough, prepared and most importantly, we have to do our best to remain positive and try to see every obstacle in our life as an opportunity in disguise.

We have to look at life from the right perspective. Instead of focusing on the negative things we must focus on the positive. When bad things happen, and they will, we have to work hard to remain positive. Look for the learning and growing opportunities that might be presenting themselves.

In Black & White

What problems are you dealing with that might be opportunities in disguise? If we're ready to recognize it, the obstacles we face can be life's way of teaching us something or pushing us in the right direction. Are you ready?

Three major obstacles I'm facing right now are:

_____

_____

_____

How can I turn these obstacles into opportunities?

_____

_____

_____

"Reflect upon your present blessings, of which every man has plenty; not on your past misfortunes, of which all men have some."– **Charles Dickens**

CHAPTER 14

Adopt an Attitude of Gratitude

Today is November 16th and surprise, surprise, its grey. In fact it's been grey for two weeks straight! I always struggle with my mood at this time of the year. The days get shorter, the weather gets colder and the sun seems to make fewer and fewer appearances. It is pretty easy to get depressed. For those of you who have a predisposition to fluctuating moods, long winter nights can be tough.

When I was in the hospital waiting for a transplant, I was initially very angry. I cried "woe is me" and "life isn't fair" for weeks. Then everything changed one day. I ran out of tears and energy. I realized that I had to find another way to cope with my struggles. I began to look at things with an attitude of gratitude.

I started making time each day to consider what I had to be thankful for. I tried to focus my mind on being grateful rather than feeling sorry for myself. Over time, my attitude about my situation changed. I wasn't magically better and I wasn't suddenly happy to be in the hospital but my life certainly didn't seem as bad as it had a few weeks before.

I began to realize that as tough as things were, I still had a lot to be thankful for. I had family and friends who loved me, I had the good fortune to live in a country with the medical knowledge to save my life and where those resources were accessible to everyone.

WHEN SOMETHING GOES WRONG IN YOUR LIFE YOU CAN THINK, "WHY IS THIS HAPPENING TO ME?" OR YOU CAN BE THANKFUL

As I began to direct my focus toward what I had to be thankful for rather than what I had to be upset about, the issues I was facing seemed to shrink.

I like to say that we should try to adopt an Attitude of Gratitude rather than thinking we should have a Life without Strife. As an upper-middle class North American, it is easy for me to take all of the blessings in my life for granted. Such things as clean running water, a warm home and secure roof over my head I take as a given. Many people in the world are not so fortunate.

So when something goes wrong in your life you can choose to think, "Why is this happening to me?" Or you can be thankful that you haven't had to face so many other things. The choice is yours.

Try an attitude of gratitude. Try focusing on your blessings and feeling grateful for what you have. When you focus on what you have to be thankful for an amazing thing happens, you discover that you have more and more of those things.

In Black & White

A great tool to help you build awareness of all of the things you have to be thankful for is a thankfulness journal.

To those of you who have never kept a journal, be forewarned; journaling isn't always easy. Some days you'll feel more creative and you'll be able to recount significant events easily. Other days you may not have the energy or memory. All you'll manage is a few point form notes. That's fine. The point is not how you do it, just that you do it.

Not only is the process of writing down the things you're thankful for good for you, but on days when you feel down or lonely or that life isn't fair, a quick read through a few pages of your journal will remind you of just how fortunate you are and help brighten your mood.

List 5 Things You Have to be Thankful For:

_____

_____

_____

_____

_____

"Adversity has the effect of eliciting talents, which in prosperous circumstances would have lain dormant."
– Horace

CHAPTER 15

Cherish Your Struggles

Initially the title of this chapter may seem to run contrary to your common sense. After all, we all hate to struggle. Dealing with difficulties in life can be scary, frustrating and exhausting. No one looks forward to going through one of life's rough patches, but we should.

I haven't mastered this yet, but I'm certainly trying. I try to embrace the challenges I face in my life rather than curse them. The reason for this is simple. I've found over and over again that my struggles against the obstacles I face are my biggest teachers and offer the greatest opportunities for self-improvement.

Like all of us, I have many struggles in life. One of my biggest struggles is living with the knowledge that my transplant will not last forever. I live each day with the knowledge that someday, probably sooner rather than later, my transplanted organs will fail. The average lifespan of transplanted lungs is somewhere between three and five years. I just celebrated the five-year anniversary of my transplant.

IT IS YOUR STRUGGLES, NOT YOUR SUCCESSES, THAT MAKE YOU WHO YOU ARE; CHERISH THEM

If the statistics are accurate, I am not likely to live to see my fortieth birthday. That said I realized a long time ago that I couldn't lead a productive and happy life if I constantly worried about when I would die. So I do my best not to think about it. But I fail sometimes. Every once in a while it hits me that if my wife and I have children I probably won't be around to see them graduate high school. I won't live long enough to retire. I won't have grandchildren.

I deal with this is by remembering that every obstacle in our life can teach us something. There is something to be learned from every seemingly negative experience. So I look at my shortened life expectancy as an opportunity to remember to live each day more fully.

Life is a journey but not in the traditional sense of the word. Unlike the wise men's journey to Bethlehem or a runner's journey to a finish line, life's journey is not about the destination, it's about the journey itself.

Life's journey is like a vacation to a foreign country or a great meal at a five-star restaurant. We don't do these things for what we get at the end; we do them for the experience. Life's isn't about getting from Point A to Point B, unless Point A is one state of being, and Point B is a more evolved state of being.

Rather than thinking of life's hurdles as obstacles that we have to leap over or find a way around in order to get to the finish line, think of them like the waves of an ocean that crash on the rocks and slowly shape them into what they will become. It is your struggles, not your successes that make you who you are. Cherish them.

In Black & White

You will face challenges in your life. You will struggle. These are facts of life. It's important to understand that struggling isn't a sign of failure; it's a side effect of being alive. If you're struggling it's because you're being shaped into a better, more compassionate human being.

Spend time this week making a list of the three things that you're struggling with right now. Examine each problem to see if you can find a hidden opportunity. Ask yourself:

- What can this issue/problem teach me about myself?
- Why am I facing this problem? Was there something that I could or should have done to avoid it?
- Do I face this problem, or one similar, often? What does this tell me about me?

"Any fool can criticize, condemn and complain but it takes
character and self-control to be understanding and forgiving."
– Dale Carnegie

CHAPTER 16

Empathize Rather
Than Criticize

At the start of this book I promised that I would be completely
honest with you. I have to admit that I tend to be critical at
times. I'm not always successful at seeing the best in people,
but I'm working on it.

FOCUS ON
COMPLIMENTING THE
PEOPLE AROUND YOU
RATHER THAN
CRITICIZING THEM

We've all been in situations where a perfectly normal conversa -
tion turned to criticism and/or mockery of someone. Who
among, in middle school or high school, didn't make fun of
someone for what they wore, the music they listened to or the
friends they hung out with?

As adults the criticism, may be less blatant but it's no less
harmful. Contrary to what some believe, you don't get someone

to do what you want them by criticizing the things they do that you don't like.

In truth, it's easier to get people to do what you want by making that something *they* want too. Help people to see how your way benefits them and they come around to your way of thinking. How do you do that?

Compliment people instead of criticizing them. Make those around want to spend time with you. Make them feel better about themselves. When people value your company your opinion gains value and your influence becomes more pervasive.

It's easy to criticize. We're good at finding fault with others. What's challenging but more beneficial is to empathize with people. When we seek to understand where someone is coming from, we become better partners, better leaders and better people.

In Black & White

This week try finding the best in everyone you come in contact with. Resist the temptation to jump to conclusions. Try to see their humanity. After all, there are good things about each of us. When we criticize and judge others we reduce them to their faults. If you catch yourself judging someone stop and see the person for who they really are.

Master this discipline and you'll notice a multitude of benefits. You'll have better relationships with the people in your life because you aren't criticizing them. You feel better about yourself when you are more positive.

"Criticism may not be agreeable, but it is necessary. It fulfils the same function as pain in the human body. It calls attention to an unhealthy state of things." – W. Churchill

CHAPTER 17

When Criticism Is Necessary

There is no question that constructive criticism is sometimes necessary. Without the objective eye of another to give us feedback, it's easy to think that we're doing everything right and there's no room for improvement.

Effective criticism can keep our egos in check and help us see how we can improve. Constructive criticism is one of the most effective learning tools in your arsenal. I encourage you to use it.

CONSTRUCTIVE CRITICISM IS INVALUABLE WHEN IT COMES FROM THE RIGHT SOURCE

When I was writing this book, I finished the first draft, went through it twice making corrections and fixing everything I wanted to change. Then I passed the manuscript to a few trusted and knowledgeable friends. When I got the work back, my friends had discovered numerous passages that I could improve and a host of grammatical and spelling errors that I had missed.

When I got my work back with red marks all over the pages I could have felt defeated or defensive about their criticism. But I didn't. I realized that their suggestions and critiques would make this book better for you.

Constructive criticism when it comes from the right source and is received in the right way is invaluable. In fact, it is likely the quickest route to self-improvement. If you're in a position of authority you need to help your people improve. Sometimes that means helping them see their weaknesses.

To increase the effectiveness of my presentations, I tape myself and ask other speakers and trusted friends to pick out my weaknesses. I receive and appreciate any constructive criticism they give. But the kicker is: truly constructive criticism isn't critical.

The people I turn to for advice deliver it in a way that lets me know what I need to work on without making me feel like a failure. I wouldn't go to these people for their critique if it consisted of: "that was awesome" or "that sucked". Neither comment is helpful. Good constructive criticism points out specific weaknesses and most importantly ideas on how to eliminate them.

In Black & White

Find someone you can trust and whose opinion matters to you to give you an honest critique. Make an appointment with this person to get an update on how you're doing every so often. A weekly, monthly or quarterly assessment of your performance can be a very helpful tool to help you succeed.

Hearing about your faults isn't easy. But successful people know that listening to criticism is essential to helping them improve. If you develop the thick skin needed to hear about what you need to improve you'll be a better partner, a better leader and a better person.

GOALS

"Great work is done by people who are not afraid to be great." – Fernando Flores

CHAPTER 18

Awaken Your Potential

Psychologists performed an experiment by putting a pane of glass in the middle of an aquarium full of water. Then they put two fish in the tank. One fish was the natural predator of the other. They put the predator on one side of the glass and the prey on the other. What happened next speaks volumes about the power of the mind.

With the glass inserted, the predator would swim quickly towards its prey and then…WHAM, it would bang into the glass. After doing this several times, the predator realized it couldn't catch the prey. The prey could swim inches from the mouth of the predator and the larger fish would do nothing because it realized that every time it tried to catch the prey fish, it hurt.

Then the scientists removed the glass from the aquarium so the fish were free to swim wherever they wished. That's where things got interesting. The prey began to swim all over the tank often passing directly in front of the predator. But the predator did nothing. It thought the glass was still there and did not want to get hurt. So it swam around doing nothing.

Think about how powerful that is. The predator was hungry, the food was swimming within inches of its mouth and the predator did nothing! Why? Two reasons: fear of pain and power of perception.

⬬

NO MATTER HOW PERFECT THE CONDITIONS ARE FOR SUCCESS, IF YOUR PERCEPTION IS THAT YOU CAN'T SUCCEED, THEN YOU CAN'T.

To Avoid Pain

The predator fish is similar to many of us. It was afraid of being hurt. In fact, it was so afraid of pain that its desire to avoid pain outweighed its desire to eat! That's a serious fear Fear may not stop us from eating but all too often it stops us from going after what we want.

The fact is we'll pass up an opportunity no matter how great if the fear of pain is great enough. It's a natural reflex. Think of a baby who touches a hot stove. Do they need to be told to take their hand off the burner once they touch it? Of course not.

They take their hand away instantly because it hurts.

Natural instincts protect us from hurting ourselves and thank God we have it But when it comes to achieving our potential, our instinct to avoid pain can be very limiting. That's why we have to find a way to deal with our fear of pain in order to achieve what we want.

The Power of Perspective

The other reason the predator fish didn't eat its prey was perception. The predator's perceived that the obstacle was still there even though the glass was removed. That was all it took to prevent the predator fish from catching its prey.

No matter how perfect the conditions for success are, if you perception is that you can't succeed you won't. Our dreams can walk right past us and we won't do a thing. Perception is 90% of reality. If we perceive that there is an obstacle in our way it doesn't really matter if the obstacle is there or not.

If you feel negatively about yourself, your life situation or your abilities, work on it. Read books on being positive. Make a list of good things that have happened or are happening in your life. Make a conscious effort to look for the opportunities in your life that may be "swimming" past you at this very moment.

In Black & White

You have the ability to do anything. Yes people have limits, but few reach them because perception is more limiting than abili-ties. The good news is that your perception is easier to improve than your abilities. That's why the biggest favour you can do for yourself is to realize your incredible potential.

Marianne Williamson, a personal development author, sums it up best,

*"Our deepest fear is not that we are
inadequate. Our deepest fear is that we
are powerful beyond measure. It is our
light, not our darkness that frightens
us most.*

*We ask ourselves, who am I to be
brilliant, gorgeous, talented, and famous?
Actually, who are you not to be? You are a
child of God.*
*Your playing small does not serve the
world. There is nothing enlightened about
shrinking so that people won't feel
insecure around you.*
*We were born to make manifest the glory
of God that is within us. It's not just in
some of us; it's in all of us. And when we
let our own light shine, we unconsciously
give other people permission to do the
same. As we are liberated from our own
fear, our presence automatically
liberates others."*

This week I want you to make this or another quote with a similar message your mantra. Use it as a daily affirmation.

I promise you that after a day of doing this faithfully you will feel more confident. If you continue it for the week you will begin to look at your life and your potential in broader terms and your perception will change. When that happens, and only when that happens, can you begin to realize your full potential.

*"Believe and act as if it were impossible
to fail." –* Charles F. Kettering

CHAPTER 19

If You Believe It
You Can Achieve It

There are few universal truths in life but this is one of them.
I firmly believe that there is nothing you can't achieve if you
believe completely that you can do it. Equally true and evident
in the lives of far too many people is, "If you can't believe it,
you won't achieve it." In other words; it must be true in your
mind and heart before it can come true in your life.

Belief is a powerful thing. It is much different than hoping,
dreaming or wishing. Believing you can do something means
that you *know* you can do it. You may not know *how* you're
going to do it, or *when*, but you know in your heart that you
can make it happen. When you have belief nothing can stop
you. What do you believe you are capable of?

When I was first on the transplant list, I met with the head of
the transplant team. During the meeting he explained how the
transplant process worked.

He made sure that I fully understood all of the risks involved in
the surgery. He said that if everything went as it should, I should
be able to go back to work part-time someday. That was his
ultimate goal for me.

If I had suggested that not only would I return to work but that I would start my own business as a speaker, travel all over North America helping people realize their potential, I'd write a book and that I'd run three marathons, he would never have believed me.

EXPECT MORE OF
YOURSELF THAN ANYONE
ELSE DOES

Today I shudder to think where I would be in life if I had lived within the confines of my doctor's expectations. I know they were trying to prepare me for every possibility; but if I had not decided that I was going to expect more from myself than they did, I would never have achieved half of what I have. Expect more from yourself than anyone else does.

If people in your life impose limiting expectations on you, have the courage to listen politely and ignore them. You don't have to shut these people out of your life; just don't let them impose their limiting attitude on your life.

Many of us will never achieve half of what we could because deep down we don't really *believe* that our goals are attainable or that we're worthy of the great things in life. We've bought into the lie that most of us are just ordinary folks who should do ordinary things, work at ordinary jobs and make ordinary money. There's nothing wrong with that. But if you want more and you *believe* that you can do more, there is nothing to stop you but you.

In order to achieve everything you are capable of you must *believe* that it is possible and your chances are good. Ignore the negative messages you've received throughout life.. I want to challenge you to reconsider your potential.

In Black & White

This week, consider what you believe is possible for you and your life. Look back to Chapter 1 to see what you said you would want to do if you only had a year left to live.

Now ask yourself: Do I really believe that this is possible?

Take a moment and write down the goals that you *believe* in your heart you can achieve:

_____

_____

_____

_____

You will never achieve something that you believe to be impossible. So start to focus on what you want to achieve with the mindset that it *is* possible.

"In creating the only hard thing is to begin: a grass blade's no easier to create than an oak." – James Russell Lowell

CHAPTER 20

There Is Great Power in Beginning

I want to share a very important piece of wisdom with you: You will never accomplish anything if you never start. There is great power in beginning.

Most people I know have at least a few goals for themselves. Unfortunately, the number of them who have actually done anything about their goals is far too small. Oh sure, we *think* about working on our goals. We *dream* about achieving those goals but we rarely *do* anything about them.

How often have you said to yourself, "I really should …"? Whether it was travel, work less, begin an exercise program or write a book. We've all had goals we failed to achieve for one reason or another. The reason we often fail is that we don't complete the most important step; start.

It sounds simple but sometimes starting is the hardest part. It's easy to get so overwhelmed and intimidated by the scope of what needs to be done that you just don't know what to do first.

JUST START,
THE MOTIVATION WILL FOLLOW

Another problem people encounter is that they make the mistake of thinking that action follows motivation. There's no reason that the opposite doesn't work just as well.

The problem with waiting for motivation before you start is that sometimes you just can't get motivated. Instead of waiting for the inspiration to start working on your goals, just start. If you get things going, motivation will follow.

In Black & White

This week go back to the list of goals you made in Chapter 6. Figure out what would be the first three steps that you'd have to take to accomplish each of these goals and write them down underneath the goal. For example, if your goal is to write a book, set aside an hour each day to write. Take the phone off the hook, turn the TV off and write.

Don't get tripped up by trying to figure out what the perfect first step is. Just write something down (you can always change it if you need to). In this situation, the key isn't *what* you do, just that you do *something*.

GOAL 1

a)

b)

c)

GOAL 2

a)

b)

c)

GOAL 3

a)

b)

c)

What you've just done is create your TO DO list. You now have nine things that you can DO today to start making your dreams come true. Don't allow yourself to get overwhelmed by the whole project. Pick the first thing on the list and get started!

"It is a funny thing about life; if you refuse to accept anything but the best you very often get it." – Somerset Maugham

CHAPTER 21

Accept Nothing But the Best

If you study the most successful and respected people in the world you'll find they share a similar trait; they accept nothing but the best in everything they do. They expect the best from their employees, their friends, their family and even themselves.

Why do you suppose that is? Are successful people all just a bunch of demanding jerks? Not at all. They just know that in order to be the best you first have to *expect* the best. Setting high personal and professional standards is critical for success. Yet most of us fail to do this simple, yet crucial thing to improve the quality of our lives and increase our chances for success.

Most of us are guilty of letting our standards slip over the course of our life. We begin accepting less than the best from everyone else in our lives. Once we do that, no matter how disciplined you are and how hard you are on yourself, that eventually leads to accepting less than the best from yourself.

One of my primary goals is to live in such a way that the eulogist at my funeral will be able to stand in front of everyone gathered and say with confidence, "Mark gave life everything he had. He may not have succeeded at everything but he never held back. When he died he had nothing left."

I believe the most powerful thing anyone can do to improve the quality of their life, be it related to work, a relationship or anything else is to decide that living life at any less than your very best is unacceptable.

Most don't achieve all that we are capable of in life. A major reason for that is because we make it okay to give less than our best efforts at some point along our journey. We accept mediocrity.

In my short lived teaching career I witnessed the tragic effects that low expectations have on students. Unfortunately we have developed a system of education that opts to lower standards to meet abilities rather than nurturing and developing the student's abilities to meet standards. Rather than demanding more from our students, we lower the bar so they can reach it without improving. Isn't that crazy?

Imagine if other institutions lowered standards rather than demanding that people meet them? Would you like to be treated by a doctor whose medical school lowered their standards and allowed him or her to graduate even though they didn't know everything that they should?

Would you want your city to hire a police officer even though he or she didn't know how to use their gun properly and couldn't pass fitness standards? What if the International Olympic Committee worked that way?

Imagine this scenario: John from Canada can't meet the mini -
mum high jump qualifying level. The International Olympic
Committee decides that rather than exclude John from competition, they'll lower the standard so that he can compete.
Great. Now John is included. How nice for him. Until he gets
into competition and is creamed by the other competitors who
were better from the beginning.

※

WHEN YOU RAISE YOUR
STANDARDS, MORE OFTEN
THEN NOT, OTHERS WILL
RISE TO MEET THEM

Now what happens if the IOC tells John that if he can't compete until he meets the standards? What does John do? He has
two choices: he can either quit (and certainly some people
would choose this option) or he can push himself to improve.

Let's assume that John chooses to raise his game. He trains
harder, improves his focus, fuels his burning desire to get to
the Olympics and four years later he comes back stronger,
faster and better. This time he qualifies on his merit. John gets
a greater sense of accomplishment because he *earned* his spot
instead of it being given to him. When he gets to the games he's
better equipped to compete.

What would happen if we all lived our lives with higher
standards? How much better could you be at everything in
your life if you decided to adopt that kind of standard for
yourself?

At the beginning of this chapter I suggested you not only demand higher standards of yourself but of those around you as well. Why? Because surrounding yourself with quality motivated people working towards their goals will help you raise your game. When you raise your standards, more often than not, others will rise to meet them.

Ask players who played with Michael Jordan, Wayne Gretzky or Joe Montana. They'll tell you that playing with these players, made them better. That's why demanding the best from those around you is so critical.

Don't misunderstand. When I say that you should accept nothing but the best from those around you I don't mean that you should be unforgiving and expect perfection all the time. That's not possible. We're human. We make mistakes. We can't expect to succeed every time. That's not what expecting the best means.

Expecting the best means expecting the best *effort* every time. People will not succeed 100% of the time but they can give 100% effort all the time. If they don't you need to call them on it of find other associates. Keep your standards high and you'll become all you can be.

In Black & White

Perfection isn't possible. Perfect effort is. Take a serious look at yourself and those you work with, play with and love this week. Evaluate the effort both you and those around you are making. If it isn't 100%, it's time to bump up your game. After all, a life lived half-assed is a life half-lived.

"The limits of the possible can only be defined by going beyond them into the impossible." – Arthur C. Clarke

CHAPTER 22

Anything Is Possible... Really

Remember when you were 5?

Remember how you believed that anything was possible? You thought that you could be and do anything. You may have even thought you could fly. Then somewhere along the way you started to lose your faith in possibilities. Subconsciously or otherwise, you absorbed the negative messages around you that said, "You can't", "you won't" and "it's not possible".

We are all capable of more than we know. But when we lose our sense of the possible and begin to believe the negative messages of our world, it can become a self-fulfilling prophecy. We believe we can't so we can't. Not only do we fail to reach our potential, we stop trying.

The good news is the self-fulfilling prophecy can work in the positive direction too. Henry Ford said, "Whether you believe you can, or you believe you can't, you're right." If you can get to a place where you honestly believe that ANYTHING is POSSIBLE, then for you, anything will be.

We all have times in our lives when it is difficult to believe that anything is possible. Life is discouraging sometimes and there are times when it feels more like NOTHING is possible. When

I go through those times I find it helpful to remember the story of Roger Banister.

IF YOU CAN GET TO A
PLACE WHERE YOU
HONESTLY BELIEVE THAT
ANYTHING IS POSSIBLE,
THEN FOR YOU,
ANYTHING WILL BE

For those unfamiliar with his name, Roger Banister was the first man to run the mile in under four minutes. He ran that distance faster than anyone ever had.

Obviously he was a very gifted and talented athlete, but that's not what made Banister special. Bannister's greatest achievement wasn't his record-breaking time; it was his ability to believe that anything is possible.

Roger Banister broke the 4:00 minute mile mark in 1954. For nearly a decade the world record held at 4:01.4. Hundreds of athletes had tried and failed to break the magic 4-minute barrier.

The 4-minute mile gained such lore that some medical professionals declared it physically impossible for a human to run it any faster. In less than four magic minutes, Bannister redefined what was possible. But that's not the end of the story. The lesson for us all is found in what happened in the months after Bannister broke the record.

While the previous record of 4:01.4 stood for nine years, in the ten years after Bannister broke 4 minutes the record was broken FIVE times. The previously elusive four-minute mark was broken several more times than that! John Landy bettered the record by a full second just one month later!

So what was so special about Landy, Derek Ibbotson, Herb Elliott and Peter Snell who all broke the four minute mark after Bannister? What did they have that the athletes who came before them didn't? They had Roger Bannister to follow.

Those runners *knew* they could reach their goal. They didn't need the vision that Bannister had because when Bannister ran the first sub-four-minute mile, he made the impossible possible!

What's the lesson for you and me? We are not likely to break running records. If we want to become all that we can be in our lives, we have to be like Roger Bannister. We have to believe that anything is possible.

When I decided that I was going to run a marathon it was only seven days after my transplant. I was forty pounds under - weight, had five chest-tubes jutting from my sides, had more than thirty staples holding together an incision that spanned the width of my chest and I hadn't run more than a few feet in several years.

If I'd told my doctors that day that I was going to run a marathon one day they would have laughed. They may have said that it was impossible. But I knew that it was possible. I knew that I could do it. It took more than two years and a lot of hard work and training, but I did it.

Whatever your goals are and whatever you want to accomplish, whether it's learning to water ski or to be the first person to walk on Mars, if you're going to succeed you must first believe that it's possible. Once you clear that mental hurdle, anything is possible… really!

In Black & White

Today, I challenge you to look at everything through the eyes of your five-year-old self and believe that anything is possible. Make a list of the things you really want to achieve in your life, even ones that you may have written off as being impossible.

Take a moment to think about why you decided that dream or ambition was impossible. Write down the excuse that you used to justify giving up on that goal. Then, for each excuse you made for why you couldn't accomplish these goals, find a solution.

Once you can see there is a solution to every obstacle that stands in your way, you'll be left with no more excuses for not getting everything you want in your life.

Now comes the last, but most important, step; take action. Do something today to start realizing one of those previously impossible dreams. And don't forget to pause for a minute, and realize how amazing you are. After all, you are about to do the impossible!

What I want to achieve:

_____

_____

_____

_____

Why Haven't I Done It Yet? :

_____

_____

_____

_____

Solutions to My Excuses:

_____

_____

_____

_____

*"Dream no small dreams for they have no power to move
the hearts of men"*
– J.W. von Goethe

CHAPTER 23

Go Big or Stay Home

The reason many people fail to reach their potential is because they allow themselves to be ruled by what other people tell them is reasonable or realistic to expect from their lives. Instead, they need to follow what they know in their heart is possible for their lives. I encourage you to do what my dad always told me to do, "Go Big or Stay Home."

FORGET REASONABLE;
THINK POSSIBLE!

Being able to fulfill your ultimate potential isn't easy. In order to do it effectively, you must be able to see whatever you want to achieve as being real and believe in your heart that you can make it happen. This week I want you to make this simple phrase your mantra:

Forget Reasonable; Think Possible! Go Big or Stay Home!

I've spent the last several years of my life trying to live out a promise that I made to myself when I waited for my transplant. To never dream small. But I failed the other day.

I was reading a great book to help me improve as a motivational speaker. Near the beginning of the book a page asked for my yearly financial goal. I *should* have written a big number. I should have gone big and written down a number that would be truly amazing. I should have but I didn't. Instead I wrote down a figure that I thought would be reasonable, something that I was fairly sure I could achieve.

What's wrong with that? Everything. The point of setting a goal is to push yourself to strive harder and farther than you think you can. By setting a small goal I made it acceptable to do less.

Remember when you were five years old? Remember what it was like when you believed in everything? You believed in Santa Claus, you believed your parents were flawless, and knew the answer to everything. Remember when you gave everyone the benefit of the doubt and assumed you could do anything?

Do you still feel that way? If you do, awesome! If not, I want you to think about why? I don't know you personally but I know that you almost certainly lost your belief in eternal possibility very slowly. You likely lost it so gradually that you didn't even notice.

Over the course of your childhood you heard things like: "No", "You Can't", and "You Shouldn't" and ever so slowly you started to lose faith in possibility. You came to believe that there are some things that just aren't possible. That's too bad.

Throughout life we are programmed to believe there are some things that are just not possible and a whole lot of things are not 'realistic' or 'likely'. We start to learn that failure hurts and humiliation hurts more.

Eventually we realize that we can minimize the chances of experiencing pain if we lower our expectations. If we dream smaller or stop dreaming altogether we can almost completely avoid the pain of failure. So we stop shooting high. That's fine for a while. Many people don't realize is that making that decision doesn't avoid the pain, it just puts it off.

Sure, if you stop going big you avoid the initial pain of failing to reach your goal or the humiliation of being mocked for the goals you have. But all you really do is postpone that pain. Later, maybe a year or 10 or maybe 30, you'll experience a different pain. This one is far worse because it lasts longer. It's called regret.

Talk to anyone who experienced the pain of regret. They'll tell you that the pain of never having tried something is far worse than the pain that comes from trying and not succeeding. I'll bet that if you look deep enough, you'll find things that you want that you've already scratched off your mental "to-do" list and labeled impossible.

In Black & White

This week your task is simple but not easy. I want you to go back to your list of goals and tell yourself over and over and over again, "This IS possible!" Say it as many times as it takes for you to believe it.

*"Unless commitment is made, there are only promises
and hopes… but no plans."*
– Peter Drucker

CHAPTER 24

Make a Decision
& Commit to It

People flip coins, others make pro and con lists and some ask their friends and family members for opinions. A few even ask the magic eight ball.

We all have made the big decisions of our lives in different ways. Any method that works for you is fine. We're all different. I want you to promise yourself today that once you make the decision you commit to it 100%.

> There's a riddle that goes like this: There are
> 3 birds on a wire. One of the birds decides to fly
> away. How many birds are left? Did you say
> two? Wrong. There are three. "But one bird left!"
> you're thinking. No. One bird *decided* to leave.
> Deciding to leave and leaving are two different
> things.

So often we decide to take action to improve ourselves and become more successful. But we fail because we never go beyond making a decision to actually *doing* something.

Other times we don't even make a decision. We are paralyzed by the fear of making the wrong decision and opt not to decide at all. What we don't realize is that by not making a decision, we effectively ensure that it will never happen.

ALL THE VISION AND ENTHUSIASM IN THE WORLD DON'T MEAN A THING IF YOU DON'T HAVE COMMITMENT

In my early 20's I was horrible at making decisions. I would waffle for days, weeks and sometimes months. It depended on the seriousness of the decision. Worst of all, after finally making a decision, I'd almost always change my mind or regret the decision. This decision-making process was not only inefficient; it prevented me from being as effective as I could have been.

Have you ever made a New Year's resolution? Have you ever stuck to one? If you're answers to those questions were "yes" and "no" you've experienced what happens when you make a decision but lack commitment. The truth is, all the vision and enthusiasm in the world don't mean a thing if you don't have commitment.

One of my speaking business heroes, Joe Calloway, put it in a way that I think is easy to understand. He says all we really have to do is "decide to go". In other words, we just have to make a conscious commitment that we are going to do whatever it is we want to do and then do it. It's really that easy.

Whether it's our career, a diet, a relationship or a fitness pro-gram, if we fail to commit, we fail every time. With commitment the effort needed for success becomes automatic and everything else falls into place.

In Black & White

What have you decided to do but haven't committed to yet? Have you "decided to go" yet?

Go back to your list of goals from Chapter 2. Have you really committed to achieving those things or were they just something to fill in the space at the end of the chapter? If you haven't committed to those goals yet, do it now. If there are things on the list that you aren't committed to cross them off. If you aren't committed to them you won't achieve them anyway.

Now take the goals left on your list and decide that you are going to work on these things continuously until you achieve them. Decide to go! If you can make that kind of commitment you'll succeed every time.

The Goals I'm committed To Achieving Are:

_____

_____

_____

_____

"Content makes poor men rich;
discontent makes rich men poor."
– Benjamin Franklin

CHAPTER 25

Be Content But Never Be Satisfied

This may be tough to understand. You may ask yourself; don't content and satisfied mean the same thing? Not really.

Contentment is something we should all strive for. As far as I'm concerned, to be content is to be able to be happy in the life you live; to be able to be grateful for what you have and enjoy life. I'm content but I'll never be satisfied.

To say that you're satisfied with everything in your life is a way to justify giving up on your dreams. I believe that if you feel completely satisfied with everything in your life, you haven't set the bar high enough. You've given in to the temptation to accept mediocrity. You've settled for being good rather than striving to be great. I encourage you not to allow yourself to be completely satisfied with your life. I believe the only time you should allow yourself to stop striving to be better is when you're six feet under.

In April 2001 I was forced to live in a hospital while I waited for a transplant. Being stuck in a hospital room smaller than some people's bathrooms for an indefinite period of time at

22 years old, was as close to a living nightmare as I'd ever experienced. There was so much I still wanted to do, so much I wanted to accomplish and at the time I wasn't sure I'd ever get to do any of those things.

I LEARNED TO STOP FOCUSSING ON WHAT I DIDN'T HAVE AND STARTED APPRECIATING EVERYTHING I DID HAVE

Initially I felt like I was wasting time, sitting in a hospital room with my life on hold waiting for a transplant that I wasn't sure would ever come. While I maintained hope that a donor would be found in time, I knew that I may never leave that hospital room. I knew that I may just be waiting to die. It was incredibly frustrating and I was far from satisfied with my life but I found contentment over a of six- month period.

I learned to stop focusing on what I didn't have and to appreci - ate everything I did have; family, friends and a relationship with God. I accepted what I couldn't change and focused on the things that I could. I found contentment but I was never satisfied.

I wasn't satisfied with being stuck in a hospital room when all of my friends were out living their lives, going to school, getting jobs and having fun.

I wasn't satisfied with the idea that while many people get seventy or eighty years to live life, I might only have twenty-three and die without doing so many of the things I wanted to do in life, like get married and have a family.

I think we all need to strive to feel content in our lives and to be grateful for what we have. But that doesn't mean that you need to be satisfied with things and stop striving to improve your life and the lives of those around you.

In Black & White

If Rosa Parks had been satisfied blacks might still sit in the back of buses. If Terry Fox had been satisfied with living with his cancer, many who have survived the disease since would be dead. Being satisfied is just an excuse for not working hard to improve and there is no excusing that.

Take a few minutes at the end of each day this week to be thankful for what you have. Also think about the things that you still want to achieve. That way you can work on finding contentment while you avoid falling into the trap of feeling satisfied.

"Only when we are no longer afraid do we begin to live."
– Dorothy Thompson

CHAPTER 26

Fear Is For Failures

Stop Being Afraid and Reach for your Goals

Are you allowing fear to hold you back? Do you need to let go of a fear or anxiety so that you can succeed?

Unfortunately, most of us don't live our lives as fully as we could because we allow our fears to limit us. We're afraid to fail, to mess up or to make the wrong decision. Don't let this happen to you. You deserve better.

Sometimes we think people who live life to the fullest are never afraid. Spend some time with those who really live life and you'll discover that they have fears just like the rest of us. They just don't let their fears rule their decisions. They don't allow fear to limit them. They don't let their fears run the show. They acknowledge the fear and then act anyway. One of my favourite examples of someone who does this well is Barbara Streisand.

Barbara Streisand is one of the greatest vocal performers of all time. She has thirty platinum albums, is second in the all-time charts with fifty gold albums (ahead of the Beatles and Rolling Stones) and perhaps most impressive, is the top-selling female artist of all time.

With all of these accomplishments, one would think Streisand would be one of the most confident performers anywhere, but she's not. In fact, Streisand suffers from horrible stage fright.

**IF YOU SPEND TIME WITH
THOSE WHO REALLY LIVE
LIFE, WHAT YOU'LL
DISCOVER IS THAT THEY
HAVE FEAR LIKE THE
REST OF US, THEY JUST
DON'T LET THEIR FEARS
RULE THEIR DECISIONS**

She's been known to get violently ill before a show. But she's built an incredibly successful career touring the world performing for tens of thousands of people.

She could have given up her dream and found another profession. She could have allowed fear to rule her actions but she didn't. She faced her fears and forged an amazingly successful career as a result.

We all deal with fear in our lives. It's a universal part of the human experience.

The fears may vary in nature and severity but we're all afraid of something. For example, many people fear public speaking. A common question I'm asked about my job is, "How do you get up in front of all of those people? Aren't you nervous?" Of course I am. You might not notice it (I hope you don't) but I'm nervous.

For me the fear of being on stage isn't stage fright. It's fear of embarrassment. In my speaking business, I share personal stories with my audiences. To connect with people, I try to be as open and authentic as I can. The problem with being honest is that it demands great vulnerability. There are few things more frightening than standing before an audience, baring your soul and hoping they'll accept you.

I face fear every time I go to work but it's worth it to me. That could have me searching for a different career but it doesn't. The way I see it, I have two choices. I can let the fear rule my decisions and find a new profession or I can decide to face my fears.

Whatever your fear, it's likely that you avoid situations where you might face it. If you suffer from the fear of speaking in public, I'm sure you aren't the first to raise your hand to volunteer to give a presentation at work. But I think you should be. Instead of shying away from the things you're afraid of, I encourage you to face them. It isn't easy, but if you sum up the courage to face your fears, an amazing thing happens. They shrink. If you're courageous enough to repeatedly face your fears they eventually disappear.

In Black & White

It's natural to have fears in life. It's common to doubt whether or not we're heading on the right path. If you're going to realize your potential and make your dreams come true, you can't allow your fears to determine your destiny.

Put your fears aside for a minute. Now that your fear is out of the way, without hesitation think, "What is my dream?" The question may take five seconds or five days to answer. Take as long as you need.

Once you have an answer write it down here:

_____

_____

_____

Now you have a dream to work toward, get started! Take action to start you on your way. Don't allow self-doubts to creep in. Gain as much momentum as you can. That way, if the fear returns you'll be ready.

Finally, make a promise to yourself. Decide right now that you aren't going to let your fears get in the way of living the life you want to live. Fears can be powerful and some people allow them to rule their life. Promise yourself today that you will never be one of those people. Live your life on your terms, and leave your fears behind!

HABITS

"We first make our habits, and then our habits make us."
– John Dryden

CHAPTER 27

You Are Your Habits
What You Do and Say Each Day
Will Determine the Quality of Your Life

From a physical perspective you may be what you eat. From a quality of life perspective you are your habits.

Behaviorists and others who study success and human behav-iour will tell you the difference between those who succeed and those who don't comes down to what they repeatedly do; their habits. If you have habits that are conducive to success you will succeed. If your habits are self-destructive, well…

As you read this chapter think about what your most pervasive habits are. But before you begin, make sure you remember what a habit really is. A habit is something that we do almost sub-consciously because it is so much a part of who we are. You look for significant behaviors rather than activities. For example, while you brush and floss your teeth every day, it isn't the kind of habit you're looking at here.

Take five to ten minutes and list your five most positive habits.

My Positive Habits

1. _____

2. _____

3. _____

4. _____

5. _____

Now that you've listed what you think are your five most positive and productive habits, it's time to look at the other side of the coin. Take a few more minutes to think about your five most negative or self-destructive habits:

My Negative Habits

1. _____

2. _____

3. _____

4. _____

5. _____

Now look at your two lists. I started this chapter by saying that you are your habits. What do your habits say about you? Are you ruled more by the habits in the first list or the second?

IN ORDER TO MAKE A CHANGE IN YOUR LIFE, YOU HAVE TO CHANGE THE THINGS YOU DO EACH DAY

Are you a smoker? Do you drink too often? Are you dependable? Are you polite and understanding? As you go through this chapter ask these kinds of questions..

You develop some habits intentionally (you don't go the gym 5 days a week by accident.) However, take inventory of your habits and you may discover some unwanted habits have crept into your life unintentionally.

Many of us want to change our lives in some way. Maybe you want better relationships, to be more successful in your career, to feel more fulfilled, have more energy or be more physically fit.

Whatever your goals are, the secret to achieving them is to real - ize that in order to make a change in your life you have to change the things you do each day. If you are what you repeatedly do then, you have to change what you repeatedly do to change who you are. As Einstein said, "Insanity is doing the same thing and expecting a different result."

Think about what you really want to achieve in your life. What is that big goal or dream that you want to achieve? Now look at your bad habits. Which of these daily actions hinders you from achieving what you want?

Similarly, look at your good habits. What could you do in addition to what you already do that will bring you closer to your objective? Do something as simple as eliminating one bad habit and replace it with a good one. You can change your course dramatically. Let's look at an example:

Pretend for a moment that one of your goals is to lose unwanted pounds. When you evaluate your habits, you discover that you: seldom eat breakfast, often snack late at night, skip the gym more often than you go and eat fast food three or four times a week. What does that tell you?

With this simple inventory you can quickly see why you haven't succeeded thus far. More importantly, you know what you have to change. If you simply replace one of your bad habits with a good one, like eating breakfast instead of skipping it, you'll be on the path to achieving your goal.

Note that I said *replace* a bad habit with a good one. It is easier to replace a habit than it is to eliminate one. So if you're trying to stop snacking while you watch television, do a crossword or fold laundry while you watch. Better yet, replace snacking and watching TV with going for a walk.

When I decided to run a marathon in 2002, I didn't get up the next day and do it. I had to train. To do that I had to develop a habit of running consistently. Running once or twice a week wasn't going to cut it. I needed to run often. So I got in the habit of running four or five times per week. Every Tuesday, Wednesday, Saturday and Sunday you could find me putting in miles out on the road. That replaced my old habit of watching

TV after dinner with going for run. It was a battle to get myself to do that at first but as time passed it became easier.

Now, exercise is a habit, a regular part of my life. I fought the internal battle to get motivated and get out on the road and now it's become a habit. It's automatic.

In Black & White

The good news and bad news of this chapter are the same: you are what you repeatedly do. If you are happy with how your life is going so far, pat yourself on the back, you've done well. If you aren't happy with how your life is going I'm sorry to say you're responsible for that too. So take responsibility and do something.

Select one of the bad habits that you put on your list and think of a positive habit that you'd like to adopt to replace it. Psychologists say that it only takes thirty days to form a habit, so stick with it for a month. While it may be tough, you soon won't even have to think about it.

Successful people are not successful by accident. They succeed because they realize that they are their habits. They choose habits that are productive and in-line with their goals.

Everything you do either brings you closer or farther away from your goals. Your challenge this week is to examine your habits and discover which ones lead you toward your goals and which prevent you from achieving what you want. Then replace the bad habits with more productive ones. Sounds easy, but it's not. Good luck.

Negative Habit:

_____

_____

Positive Habit to Replace It:

_____

_____

*"Perseverance is a great element of success. If you only knock
long enough and loud enough at the gate, you are sure to
wake up somebody."*
– H.W. Longfellow

CHAPTER 28

Work Hard

One of the biggest differences between the most successful people in the world and those who just get by, is what the successful people do after everyone else goes home. Finding the energy to give just a little more effort is often the difference between failure and success.

Most people sell themselves short. They expect little from themselves and guess what they get? They're content to coast along rather than push themselves to give a little more. Don't be one of those people.

More than seventy-five years after his death, Thomas Edison is still considered one of the most successful inventors in history. He has over a thousand patents registered to his name; he's prolific to say the least.

Many people don't know that Edison was not a success because of a God-given natural ability. Inventing did not come any easier to him than anyone else. He worked hard and struggled continuously to improve and find solutions. When he was working on the technology that would result in the light bulb he completed ten-thousand failed experiments! TEN THOUSAND!

⫸

THE DIFFERENCE BETWEEN THE GREAT SUCCESSES OF THE WORLD, AND EVERYONE ELSE, IS THAT THOSE WHO SUCCEED ARE WILLING TO DO WHAT EVERYONE ELSE ISN'T

Think about the determination that must have taken. How many of us give our dreams even three failed attempts before we quit? What would happen if you were able to find the kind of determination that Edison possessed? What if you gave your dreams just 10 tries or even 5?

No matter how tired and frustrated you are you can always give a little bit more. The difference between the successes of the world and everyone else is that those who succeed are willing to do what everyone else isn't. They're willing to make the sacrifices, put in the time, and give the effort necessary for success.

In Black & White

If you want to ensure your own success, make the decision that you are going to be willing to do whatever it takes to achieve what you want in your life. When I say that you should do whatever it takes I mean that, barring breaking the law, you will stop at nothing to get what you want.

When you can give your goals and dreams that kind of commitment there is nothing you can't accomplish. When you tire and lose your drive, and you will, dig deep and find the energy to make that final push. It's that final push that most people aren't willing to make that separates the good from the great!

*"Every man who knows how to read has it in his power to
magnify himself, to multiply the ways in which he exists, to
make his life full, significant and interesting."*
– Henry Huxley

CHAPTER 29

Read

It's been said that if you read about any topic for just one hour
a day every day, after five years you'll know as much about that
topic as anyone; imagine that. Five years from now you could
be an expert in something that you hardly know anything
about right now. What would happen if you applied this rule to
something you already know something about? What if you
spent that amount of time reading about your company, your
industry or your dream career?

What if you set aside an hour a day to read: mission state -
ments, annual reports, and anything else that your company
puts out to the public, its employees and investors? In five
years you would know as much about the place you work as
the CEO. What would that knowledge do for your career?
What would it do for your bank account? What could it do for
your quality of life?

I can hear some of you whining already. But I hate to read! I
don't have the time! My answer to you is simple; do it anyway!

I am by no means an avid reader. I was an English major in university. I had to read so much that for a long time after graduating I didn't read anything more than the occasional Readers Digest article. But over time I've developed what I consider one of the most crucial elements to my success; the discipline of daily reading.

READING MAY BE THE CHEAPEST THING YOU CAN DO TO MAKE YOURSELF MORE EFFECTIVE

Reading, like eating vegetables, I did at first only because I knew it was good for me. Over the years, I've grown to enjoy it. Now I wouldn't consider going more than a few days without reading something of consequence.

When I decided on a career in the motivational speaking industry I had no idea where to start. I went to the Internet, did a search and found hundred of websites, articles and books about speaking. I devoured as many of them as I could. While merely reading about something doesn't replace hands-on experience, you can still learn a lot. That reading gave me a great start and helped me to figure out what I had to do in order to get started in the business.

Reading may be the cheapest thing that you can do to make yourself more effective in your personal and professional life. Maybe you're asking yourself, if reading is so powerful, why isn't everyone doing it? The answer is simple; it takes time and dedication, things that many people aren't willing to give. Being great in life requires being willing to do what others aren't. What choice will you make?

In Black & White

What are you waiting for? Start today. If you can't find an hour all at once read for fifteen minutes now and then. Get books on tape and listen to them on your commute. Any time you can devote is better than none.

Go check out your local book store or library today. They're great places to hang out and they have a plethora of great reading material.

Get a book and start reading. Call me in five years and tell me what you've learned. The statistics say you'll be an expert in your field; I'll want to learn from you!

"Prayer does not change God,
but changes him who prays."
– Soren Kierkegaard

CHAPTER 30

Pray

This book is nondenominational. My faith is a very important part of my life but I will not push my religion on you. How - ever, I advocate prayer because I believe whether you pray to God, Allah, Vishnu, or Mother Earth, your life will be better if prayer is a part of it. Spending time in silent reflection and having reverence for something greater than yourself is a useful tool to help you remember what really matters.

Prayer is a comforting exercise. When I sit quietly in prayer, I get a sense of connection with the world around me and with a world not of this world. To realize that I'm just a dot on a planet that's a dot in a galaxy that's a dot in the universe puts my problems in perspective in a powerful way.

Prayer also keeps me humble. It can be easy in our moments of greatest success to feel powerful, amazing and even self-righteous. We feel like we can do anything and that we're 100% responsible for all that has gone right with our lives. We might even take credit for the good things going on in the lives of others, our community or the world if we feel grandiose enough.

My belief is that we are nothing without God. I would literally not exist if it were not God's will that I exist. And so I owe him everything!

HAVING REVERENCE FOR SOMETHING GREATER THAN YOURSELF WILL HELP YOU REMEMBER WHAT REALLY MATTERS

Shortly after my transplant I sank into a severe depression. I couldn't get excited about anything. I had no energy. I had no interest in doing things that used to entertain me. It was all I could do just to get out of bed each morning.

For the first time in my life I had serious thoughts of suicide. More than scared, I felt helpless, aimless and without a purpose. That's when I turned to the only entity I knew I could count on, God.

For a while, the words I wanted to say wouldn't come. All I could do was read prayers and repeat the ones I'd memorized. But time passed and the healing began. Things started to turn around. While I didn't feel like myself, I knew that I wanted to live and that things would improve.

God helped my heart and soul heal over time. I found meaning in my life again. It took time, faith and patience but it happened. I found interest and passion and perhaps most importantly I found myself. I was finally "me" again.

To me, that's what prayer is for. It's the ultimate tool for creating wellbeing. You can pray when you can't do anything else. It's an incredibly powerful thing. It can do amazing things in your life: help you focus, ease anxiety and give you purpose. If you pray you know what I mean. If you don't, try it. It works.

In Black & White

Set aside some time at the beginning and end of each day for prayer. If you aren't a "religious person" you can still pray. Pray to the "god" that you believe in, or just meditate on the higher powers of the universe.

Try these ideas:

- Sit quietly in a dimly-lit room for a pre-defined period of time and allow yourself to just "be". Try not to think about anything. Empty your mind of all concerns and worries and just be at peace.
- Pray a mantra-like prayer repeatedly for five or ten minutes. Things like, "Let go and let God", or "I love you God" work well or me. Try different things until you find what works for you.
- Try setting aside time for prayer twice a day to get centered, thank God for your blessings and ask for help where you need it. Framing your day with this quiet time, will help you make the most of the time you have each day.

"Exercise should be regarded as a tribute to the heart"
– Gene Tunney

CHAPTER 31

Work Up a Sweat

I'm a runner. It started as a way to get in shape, then it became a hobby and now it's a full blown addiction. If I don't run at least three times a week it's not a good week.

I aim to run 20-40 km a week. If I can find the time, I also cross train a few times a week either lifting weights or doing core strengthening. My physical fitness is a very important part of my life. Not so much because I want to look good, although that's a part of it, but because I believe that physical success is an essential part of overall success.

Consider the successful people in the world. Whether their chosen field is medicine, business, education, and real estate those at the top are almost always physically fit.

Physical exercise has been scientifically proven to produce a host of beneficial side effects such as: stress relief, increased ability to focus, better quality of sleep, improved mood and longer life span.

Physical activity not only keeps your waistline in control, it keeps you in control. It doesn't just keep you busy, it helps keep you healthy, happy and productive.

PHYSICAL SUCCESS IS AN ESSENTIAL PART OF OVERALL SUCCESS

Besides the direct physical and psychological benefits of exer-cise there are a number of unseen and cumulative effects of exercise that are beneficial. For example, the sense of accomplishment and self-mastery that comes from completing an exercise program is incredible. Do you remember how you felt when you learned how to ride a bike, swim or hit a baseball?

Don't believe me? Is there a local road race coming up where you live? (If you don't know, go to www.runnersworld.com and find races in your area). Go to the race, stand at the finish line and watch people finish their race and accomplish their goals. Whether it's a marathon or a 5k, their faces will be filled with pride and accomplishment.

There is no question in my mind that the confidence acquired by gaining physical self-mastery spills over into other parts of your life. When you start to feel better physically, you'll start to feel better mentally and emotionally too. When you become a physical success you start to achieve greater success in your personal and professional life as well.

In Black & White

Quit making excusing why you still carry that extra 20 pounds. No matter what your "reasons", they're really just excuses. If you want it bad enough you can do it. So want it! Then, do it!

Find an activity of appropriate intensity.

If you've been an athlete most of your life and you recently stopped exercising, return to where you left off. Keep challenging yourself. It helps you stay interested and get the maximum benefit.

On the other hand, if you've been living on the couch for the last five years, you need to start slowly. Don't go out and try a 10km run tomorrow. Start with a daily walk of twenty or thirty minutes or go to the gym a few times a week. Take it slow to reduce the risk of injury and burnout. Set yourself up for success.

Find Something that Fits Your Personality

If you're a social butterfly don't run for half an hour alone. You'll have way too much time to think about how uncomfortable you are and your odds of success will go way down. Find a place where you can exercise and socialize at the same time. Join a club or a gym where you are surrounded by other people with the same goals.

Remember that whatever your personality-type and preferences there is an activity suited to you. There's no need to endure an activity you dislike just because you know it's good for you. Shop around until you find something that suits your lifestyle, your fitness level and your personality. Trust me, it's out there.

Just Start

Don't wait for a free day on the calendar or a sunny, warm day to get started. Conditions will never be perfect. And there is always a reason NOT to exercise, so just start! Do it today!

*"My heart, which is so full to overflowing, has often been solaced
and refreshed by music when sick and weary."*
– Martin Luther

CHAPTER 32
Sing and Dance

Right now I'm listening to Dave Matthews Band's, "Ants
Marching". There's something about it; the rhythm of the snare
drum, the licks on the electric violin; I love it. Whenever I listen
to it I become instantly more energized and more positive.

Music is a great source of entertainment. It can provide an
escape much like a good novel or a movie. But it's more
powerful than that. In fact, if you only use music for
entertainment you're missing out.

I have eclectic tastes in music. I listen to all sorts of music for
all kinds of reasons: to help me relax, to add to a celebration, to
cheer me up and to get me ready to perform and of course, to
run. To me few things are better than pulling on my shorts,
lacing up my sneakers, putting on my headphones and going
for a run.

THE MUSIC YOU LISTEN TO
CAN DO A LOT FOR YOU
IF YOU KNOW HOW TO USE IT

Research shows that music has a significant emotional and psychological impact on us. Music has been proven to help: relieve chronic pain, increase relaxation, enhance cognitive performance, improve mood, increase efficiency and accuracy and improve the quality of your work. The key is to listen to the right kind of music.

So what are you listening to? Does your music engage you, or is it just background noise? From my experience, the greatest benefit is achieved when you listen to whatever kind of music really speaks to you. So find what works for you and listen to that music as often as you can.

In Black & White

Are you listening to the right kind of music? This week I challenge you to make sure you're listening to great music. If you don't have a portable music player, get one and put some great music on it. For less than $100 you get all of the aforementioned benefits.

"Anyone who stops learning is old, whether at twenty or eighty. Anyone who keeps learning stays young. The greatest thing In life is to keep your mind young." – Henry Ford

CHAPTER 33

Learn as Much as You Can

They say you learn something new everyday. How often is that true for you?

Our lives should be growing experiences. Someone once said, "Show me a man who has stopped growing and I'll show you someone who is dead." While we recognize this to be true, continuous growth can be very challenging.

Growth is easy early in life. First we're at school where we live everyday/ then we graduate and we're out in the world on our own. Everything is new and fresh. At those points in life we learn new things without trying. But as we get older we tend to fall into routine—doing the same thing day in and day out.

Living this way makes life stale and before you know it, we are in a rut and learning new things is an increasingly rare occurrence.

Many people go through life feeling comfortable thinking they know all that they need to know. While they may realize that there are other things for them to learn they feel no need to learn them. Don't fall into that trap.

THEY SAY YOU LEARN SOMETHING NEW EVERYDAY BUT HOW OFTEN IS THAT TRUE FOR YOU?

As we age, we have to work increasingly hard to learn new things. Not because we know so much but because our drive to learn more tends to fade over time.

We don't stop learning because there's nothing left to learn. We stop learning because we stop trying to learn. At that moment we start to get old.

In Black & White

Below I list a few things that you can do to keep growing and learning. This week I challenge you to try one of these things. Once you exhaust this list, or if none of these ideas speak to you, I challenge you to make a list of your own.

Visit a new place

Try to see one new place each year. It doesn't have to be exotic, although that's certainly nice. Any place new will give you a unique experience. Wherever you go, do the "touristy stuff". Learn the history, take lots of pictures and really experience it.

Learn a new language

Most North Americans only speak one language. Some speak two, but that's rare. The ability to speak three or more languages is a special accomplishment. Become one of the rare people to accomplish this feat.

Take a Class

Take a cooking class or an art class at your local college. Most people have something that they're interested in and would like to learn more about. Set some time aside and start learning more about a language, a sport, a trade or anything you've long been curious about.

If you're really motivated, go back to school full time. As long as you're still learning, you're still growing, and if you're still growing, you're still *alive*.

"Fill your mind with the good, the clean, the pure, the power-ful and the positive." – Zig Ziglar

CHAPTER 34
Watch What You're Watching

Television has gotten a bad reputation for too long. Television, my Mom called it "the boob tube", is often blamed for child - hood obesity; a contributing factor in children's shrinking attention span and a source of over-exposure to violence. While these accusations have some merit, don't let them poison you to television.

Psychological and medical studies show that watching or listening to something funny can improve memory, increase blood flow and boost your immune system! Imagine that! You can fight the flu by watching Seinfeld! Those facts probably don't come as much of a surprise to you. We've all heard of the benefits of laughter. But how many of us put it into practice on a consistent basis?

I have long made it a habit to watch comedies and uplifting shows and movies almost exclusively. Among my favourites are: Seinfeld, Friends, The Cosby Show, National Lampoon's Christmas Vacation, Office Space and Old School. I also love films that inspire and motivate me, like: Dead Poet's Society, Mr. Holland's Opus and Rudy.

YOU ARE WHAT YOU
WATCH. PUT GARBAGE IN,
YOU GET GARBAGE OUT

In addition to watching comedy I make it a policy not to watch anything that I consider to be harmful or negative. You won't find things like: Nightmare on Elm Street, The Grudge, Hostel or any other piece of "entertainment" that focuses on the torture and killing of people in my collection. It's a frightening concept when we decide to watch killing, destruction and torture as entertainment! How messed up is that?

I'm a strong believer that in we are what we eat. We also are what we watch. In other words; put garbage in and you get garbage out. Put in horror, violence, destruction and sadness and you have to fight all that off in order to be a positive force in the world. On the other hand, put in humour, love and inspiration and it becomes much easier to put those things out into the world.

Am I suggesting that you try to live in a world of make-believe where everything is happy all of the time? Absolutely not. We have to be realistic. While there is no way to avoid exposure to negative images and messages, there is no need to expose ourselves to these things on purpose, as entertainment!

In Black & White

Watch what you watch. Pay attention to what you put in your brain. Make it a policy to watch nothing but positive and uplifting material for the next two weeks.

To see the effect this can have, track what you watch each day and how you feel. I think you'll find that eliminating negative images from your life improves your mood and attitude.

"Many are called, but few get up."
– Oliver Herford

CHAPTER 35

Get the Worm, Reach Your Goals
The Value of Rising Early

I was the only teenager I knew who got up at 7:00am—even on Saturday. Not that I was a super keen kid, I've just always been an early riser. As a child I was famous, or infamous, for being up by 6:00 am every day. I loved to get up early. My parents made a rule that I wasn't allowed in their room before 7:00 am.

Now I'm 27 years old and things haven't changed. Maybe it's 8:00 instead of 7:00 but I'm always up early. The difference is that I was up early as a kid because I couldn't sleep. Now I wake up early because I believe that it's one of the keys to success.

Getting up early allows you to act and actively engage in creative thinking when your brain is at its best. Our biological clocks are set to wake up when the run rises and sleep when the sun sets.

Since the dawn (no pun intended!) of the light bulb we stay up and get up later. We no longer depend on the sun for light. We've stretched our days, shortened our nights and the result is getting less sleep.

Many researchers argue that sleep deprivation contributes to obesity, depression, mood disorders and headaches. To combat this problem, specialists say "early to bed, early to rise."

**GETTING UP EARLY
ALLOWS YOU TO TAKE
ACTION AND BE
ACTIVELY ENGAGED IN
CREATIVE THINKING
WHEN YOUR BRAIN IS AT
ITS BEST**

If health hazards aren't enough to persuade you to hit the hay earlier tonight, consider the effect sleep has on your success. Getting up early not only gives you a jump on the day, it gives you a jump on everyone else who's sill in bed. So if you aren't already getting up by 6:30 try it.

I challenge you: Get up a half-hour earlier each day. You'll sud - denly have three and a half extra hours a week. You'll discover that you can accomplish an amazing amount before most people hear their alarms. And that feeling is a VERY good one!

There's no doubt that rising early involves sacrifice. You get up at 6:00 everyday if you stay up until 1:00 or 2:00 am every night. But as my mom once told me, "nothing good happens after 2:00 am." So get to bed at night. Give up the late nights and get up with the sunrise. Few things compare to the feeling of sitting with your morning coffee and watching the sun come up. I don't get to do it as often as I'd like, but wow, what an awesome way to start the day!

In Black & White

Tonight, get to bed a bit earlier and set the alarm ahead by a half hour. You'll be tired for a few days but you adjust. Being up before everyone else gives you a sense of possibility and accomplishment, like you have a head start on everybody else.

So start getting yourself up a little earlier this week. Within a few weeks, it will be a habit and you have a great advantage over everyone who is still asleep at 6:30.

"Think in the morning. Act in the noon. Eat in the evening.
Sleep in the night."
— **William Blake**

CHAPTER 36

Get Some Sleep

In the book "Lights Out", authors T.S. Wiley and Bent Formby discuss the collection of detrimental effects we suffer when we don't get enough sleep. Scientists and doctors say a lack of sleep can be blamed at least in part for: depression, mood swings, accidents, decreased productivity, low sex drive and weight gain, just to name a few.

Whether or not you've experienced any of these adverse effects, we all know that when we don't get enough sleep we aren't as effective as we could be. The problem is, no matter how aware we are of this on an intellectual level, we still have trouble putting that knowledge into practice.

In our busy world with our hectic lifestyles, we place so much value on getting things done, or more accurately, on being busy, that our priorities are askew. Unfortunately for many, getting a good night's sleep is the last item on our priority list.

Sleep has gone from being a valued necessity to a tolerated annoyance. Some consider it a sign of weakness. "If you can't function on 4 or 5 hours" say some, "you need to toughen up". Granted, we don't all need the same amount of sleep to feel rested, but we all need sleep.

Value your sleep. Make time for it like you do for appointments at work. Make it a priority in your life. Not just because you deserve it (although you certainly do) but because you NEED it!

**VALUE YOUR SLEEP.
MAKE IT A PRIORITY IN
YOUR LIFE. NOT JUST
BECAUSE YOU DESERVE
IT, BUT BECAUSE YOU
NEED IT**

A primary method of torture the military uses on prisoners is sleep deprivation! That's right! To TORTURE PRISONERS they KEEP THEM AWAKE!!! They know that depriving people of sleep breaks them. Their wills dissolve, their mind grows sluggish and they lose emotional control. These are great results if your goal is to get information out of a POW, but it's no way to live your life!

So why do we torture ourselves? Why don't you treat yourself better than the military treats their prisoners?

More sleep may ensure that you won't fall asleep at your desk at 3:00. Better yet, it will make you sharper, more accurate, better focused and put you in a better mood. It can also make you more patient, more positive and even thinner! That's right, rather than eating celery sticks all day, drinking 12 gallons of water and keeping track of every scrap of food that crosses your lips, try something a little simpler instead. Try sleeping!

Studies show that sleep helps keep insulin levels more balanced. This helps keep cortisone levels from making us want to pig out. In short, getting better sleep can help you become a healthier you.

One more thing. Get to bed early! Many people think that eight hours is eight hours no matter when you get them. Not true. It's better to sleep eight hours rather than four, but the time of night you sleep makes a difference. The quality of evening sleep is better than the sleep you get after midnight.

Research shows the sleep we get before midnight is more restful and restorative than after. A plus is most of us are more productive in the morning than we are in the afternoon. So you're better to sleep from 10:00pm to 6:00am than 1:00am to 9:00am (the gym is less crowded at 6:00am than at 6:00 pm too).

Our circadian rhythms are connected to the rising and setting of the sun. So our ultimate goal should be to get our schedule to match the schedule of the sun as closely as possible. So hit the pillow a little earlier tonight. You'll be sharper, healthier and more positive as a result

In Black & White

I know that getting to bed early isn't easy. I used to be a night hawk (and still am when I'm on vacation) but with a little work and good intention, you can do it.

"But I can't sleep that early" you say. Don't make a big change all at once. If you normally go to bed at midnight, don't go to bed at 10:30 tonight. You'll end up staring at the ceiling for an hour. Instead, go to bed twenty minutes earlier than your usual bedtime for a few days. Then, try twenty minutes earlier. Your body will gradually adjust and you'll be able to hit the hay at a reasonable hour.

I shoot for 10:30. That let's me sleep for 8 hrs and still be up at 6:30. If you adopt this discipline, I promise that in a few weeks you'll be more effective than before.

Now check the clock. If it's past ten, put this book down and go to sleep.

My goal wake-up time is: _____

Tomorrow I'll get up at: _____

"When I've had a rough day, before I go to sleep I ask myself if there's anything more I can do right now. If there isn't, I sleep soundly." – L Colbert

CHAPTER 37

You Can Always Sleep Tomorrow

This does not negate the previous chapter. It's another of life's dualities. As important as your sleep is, you can always sleep tomorrow. So don't ever allow yourself to miss out on a great experience or special time with friends just to ensure that you get your eight hours of shuteye. I still regret the fun times that I missed out on before I learned that lesson.

I wasn't a typical teenager. I wasn't into partying or drinking and because of my health and the medication I took, I really needed my sleep. As a result, I wasn't a regular at those weekly "gatherings" at my friend's houses. While I had lots of friends at school, when the bell rang, my life was quite different from many of my friends.

While I don't regret my decision to avoid alcohol and drugs in high school, I sometimes wish that I had accepted invitations to go to those weekend parties. I'd often get a call or an invite at school to go hang out on a Friday night and turn it down because I knew that if I went, I would be tired in the morning. Granted I had a health condition that left me more susceptible to fatigue, but I was far more cautious than I needed to be and I missed out as a result.

IF YOU FIND YOURSELF MISSING OPPORTUNITIES TO DO THINGS WITH FRIENDS JUST BECAUSE YOU DON'T WANT TO BE TIRED THE NEXT DAY, RETHINK YOUR PRIORITIES

I am a strong believer in taking care of you. That means getting your sleep, eating right and getting exercise. However, when those things interrupt LIVING, something is wrong.

If you find yourself missing opportunities to do things with friends just because you don't want to be tired the next day, rethink your priorities. You can always sleep in on Sunday.

Your life will not become what you want it to be if you constantly put off the work that needs to be done to accomplish what you want in your life. But there is no point in working to achieve things if you're not going to take the time to enjoy, celebrate and revel in those accomplishments and share them with friends and family.

In Black & White

Life is to be lived. If you find that you're too busy caring for yourself that you don't have time to LIVE your life, make changes. Ask yourself:

What am I needlessly allowing to get in the way of living my life?

"It is only by saying "no" that you can concentrate on the things that really matter." – Steve Jobs

CHAPTER 38

Just Say No

"Just Say No" means do not be afraid to tell people in your life that you don't have time for them today or that you just need a break.

Look at your schedule for the next two weeks. In addition to your commitments on the calendar, think of all the other commitments you have. Look at the necessary demands on your time: buying groceries, cleaning the house, driving kids' places, visiting family and friends, sleep and making meals.

Now estimate the time you spend on each activity. Include the time you spend at work and your commute to and from work each day. Add up these hours. Now, subtract your total from the 168 hrs in a week. This is your total "Free" time for the week.

Did you get a negative number? You may have. Double check your math. If you get a negative number, it's most likely your prioritizing needs evaluation.

If you discover in doing this exercise that you don't have enough hours in your day, you know that you have work to do. If you don't have 15 hrs of unscheduled time throughout your week, you need to find it. That may sound like a lot, but it's only 10% of your time. That's not a lot to ask is it?

IF YOU CAN FIND
TIME FOR THIS IMPORTANT
THINKING, YOU'LL SOON
DISCOVER WHAT CHANGES
YOU NEED TO MAKE, AND
BEST OF ALL, YOU'LL HAVE
TIME TO MAKE THOSE
CHANGES

Why is this 10% so important? Because great ideas and inspiration to create change come when our brain has the chance to relax and think.

When I sat in the hospital for six months, time was the greatest gift I was given. It gave me the chance to sit and think. It was during this time that I decided to become a motivational speaker. It was during this time that I began to form the ideas that would be the foundation of this book.

Have you ever met, or are you one who slugs away working 60, 70, 80 hours a week at a job they hate? Do you know someone who wants out of their job more than anything but feel they're trapped because they need the money?

Some people want to explore other avenues. They want to see what they're really capable of and know deep down that they could do something great. But they have no idea what that something is. Other times, they don't feel free to make the choice to leave it all and determine what they really want to do. What's worse, they don't have the time to figure out a way to do it.

Why? Because there aren't enough hours in their days! We live in a society that praises "busy-ness" as a grand achievement. We wear our 'busy-ness' like a badge of honour. We even compete with each other about who's the busiest. Have you ever heard a conversation like this?

"I just can't catch my breath;
I'm so busy these days!"
"I know. I'm so busy I haven't slept in weeks!"
"I must have worked sixty hours this week!"
"That's nothing! I worked eighty hours!"

Somehow, our society has decided that having something to do all the time and being too busy to sit down is a good thing. I beg to differ.

What if you had a day to do nothing but think? Wouldn't that be great? Finding a whole day may seem impossible, but keep reading and I think you'll be able to find a few hours each week to start working on shaping your life into what you want it to be.

In Black & White

Today I want you to start saying "No". I know that it's hard but you can do it. Say it with me, "No". N-O. Start practicing it wherever you go. Say "No" to the boss who wants you to work late on Friday. Say No to your kids who want to join hockey even though they're already in four other activities. Say "No" to your friends who want you to go out again this weekend. Say, "No".

Be forewarned, this can be hard at first, especially if you are a people-pleaser who craves the approval of others. It may take a few tries to get the words out. But boy does it feel good! And after you do it once it gets easier.

You obviously can't say no to everything. We all have things that we *have* to do. Bills need to get paid, meals need to be prepared and contrary to what some would have you believe, you *do* need to sleep. But chances are there are lots of things that you are spend time on that could be eliminated. That's where you can find time to work on making changes in your life.

Try this: keep saying "No" until you have at least 15 hrs to yourself each week. Do this and your schedule will open up. You'll find that you have more time to yourself, time that's critical for creative thinking and problem solving. If you can find time for the important thinking, you'll soon discover what changes you need to make. Best of all, you'll have time to make those changes!

"Every now and then go away, have a little relaxation, for when you come back to your work your judgment will be surer." – Leonardo DaVinci

CHAPTER 39

Get More Done, Go to the Beach

Logic tells us that to accomplish more, we have to work more, work harder, or both. In some cases that's true. But no matter how efficient and determined you are, you eventually get tired.

We all reach a point where we stall and just can't seem to make progress. That's why sometimes the most productive thing you can do is relax.

Take a break when you need it. Whether it's at the beach, a golf course or a yoga class, it's critical to peak performance. It offers the opportunity to take time to think, to dream, to sleep. If done right, a thirty minute break can be spiritually and mentally restorative. You don't expect your car to run for years without any maintenance. Don't expect yourself to do it either.

Part of your "maintenance" should be time to relax. Relax, decompress and just plain escape from whatever you're doing. This is often the best thing you can do to increase your creativity and productivity. All the great companies know this.

SOMETIMES THE MOST PRODUCTIVE THING YOU CAN DO IS RELAX

Internet giant Google is a great example of a company that understands the benefits of ensuring that their employees remain stress free. The company that revolutionized the way we search on the Internet treats their employees like royalty.

Here are just a few of the amazing amenities enjoyed by Google staff: five free days of childcare per year, $8000 in tuition payments, access to a sauna, dry cleaner, gyms, a gourmet cafeteria where everything is free, video games to play, a nap room and on-site oil changes are just some of the things Google does to ensure peak performance from their employees.

Why does the management Google spend so much money to ensure their staff's comfort? It seems counter-productive to encourage employees not to work doesn't it? That's not what Google does.

Google invests big bucks in their employees in these ways because they know that a happy, relaxed and comfortable employee is a productive and creative employee. They spend the money because they know it comes back to them several times over in the form of productivity, job satisfaction and dedicated employees. They know that in the long run, they will get the most out of their people by giving them the chance to be human.

Are you feeling stuck? Are you feeling burned out? If so, you're about to read three words that could change everything:
Take a Break!

Go for a walk, go to the beach or take a yoga class. If you don't have time for that at least take the time to close your eyes and take a deep breath in through your nose and out through your mouth. It's incredible how something so simple can instantly make you feel more relaxed.

When the pressure is on and you're on a deadline, it is hard to take time away from a project. For many, it takes more discipline to take a break than it does to keep going. But if you pry yourself away, even briefly, you'll come back to whatever you were doing with more fire, more passion and more focus.

Go ahead. Go to the beach. Your boss might thank you, maybe not right away, but eventually.

In Black & White

Set aside half an hour everyday this week just for you. Go for a walk, have a hot bath, read a book or do absolutely nothing at all. This little bit of time can recharge your batteries and will help you to be more productive with the other 23 ½ hours in your day.

This week I will set aside a half hour between _____ and _____ for me.

"Every time we say 'thank you', we experience nothing less than heaven on earth." – Sarah VanBreathnach

CHAPTER 40

Say Please and Thank You

So you say to yourself, "Say please and thank you"? That's your wisdom for this week? Tell me something new and exciting!" Maybe this simple habit of politeness isn't new, but it certainly isn't common. That's why I want to devote a chapter to reminding you about the importance of being polite.

Have you been to a store or restaurant where the service was horrible or where you were ignored? My aunt told me about a trip to a fast food chicken outlet (name are omitted to protect the rude) that illustrates my point.

My aunt and her family went in, stepped up to the counter and placed their order. Their order included a chicken sandwich that required preparation.

When my uncle ordered the sandwich, the cashier gave a large sigh and said, "Well, I'll *have* to check if the cook can do it." "The crazy thing was" explained my aunt, "that the cook was standing two feet away! She acted like it was a big deal to turn her head and ask him to cook that chicken sandwich!"

I laughed when I heard this. It's a sad comment on current customer service trends.

WHEN WAS THE LAST TIME YOU SAID "THANK YOU" TO SOMEONE?

An example of how rare simple manners have become happened to me this morning. I opened the door for a female co-worker. She almost fell over herself in surprise and gratitude as if I'd done something special. I think it's a sad commentary on our society when a simple act of courtesy is so rare that my coworker felt that it warranted a reaction.

Saying "please" and "thank-you" are simple things. But we shouldn't make the mistake of thinking that because they're simple that they aren't important. No matter what your goals and ambitions are, good manners will serve you well. It's amazing how far a simple heartfelt "Thank You" will get you.

A colleague tells a story in his presentations about writing a "Thank You" note for his high school principal when he was in grade twelve. He wrote the note when he graduated. When he returned to visit several years later, he found that same note was STILL on the wall.

Finding it strange that someone would keep such a simple note for so long, he asked his principal why the note was still there. His principal explained that it was so rare an event for him to get a note from a student thanking him for something, that he cherished it enough to keep it on his wall for half a decade!

When was the last time you said, "Thank You" to someone for something he or she has done for you? It is easy to take others and what they do for granted. Don't do it for another day!

In Black & White

Take a few minutes today to write a note to someone who's recently done something for you. It doesn't have to be anything major. Just think of something that someone did for you that made your day a little better and thank them. Tell them what it meant to you.

I promise you, your note will affect that person. It will make them feel noticed and appreciated. Who knows, five years from now, your note may still be on that person's wall.

FOCUS ON WHAT MATTERS

"Concentrate all your thoughts upon the work at hand. The sun's rays do not burn until brought to a focus."
– Alexander Graham Bell

CHAPTER 41

Focus

What do Fortune 500 CEOs, professional athletes and neuro-surgeons have in common beside huge salaries? Focus. If you made a list of the things that separate people who are mediocre in their field from those who are exceptional, focus would be near the top.

For many of us, we struggle with focus, consciously or otherwise. We may not be aware of it, but we have so many things going on in our lives, it can feel like we're moving in a hundred different directions at once. Getting focused is critical to success. However, anyone who tells you that it's possible to live your life focused on just one thing is delusional.

Our lives are multi-faceted. There are half a dozen aspects to life that you need to manage effectively in order to be your best. You need a focus or a goal for each of them. Don't believe me? Try letting your work life or your home life slip for a few weeks, what happens?

IF YOU MADE A LIST OF THE THINGS THAT SEPARATE THE PEOPLE WHO ARE MEDIOCRE IN THEIR FIELD FROM THOSE WHO ARE EXCEPTIONAL, FOCUS WOULD BE NEAR THE TOP OF THE LIST

Focus is essential to success because without it we become stressed trying to manage the multitude of priorities in each aspect of life that we let things fall by the wayside to preserve our sanity. The flaw with this strategy is that by trying to accomplish everything, we end up accomplishing nothing.

Don't fall into the trap of being busy doing nothing. Look at the different aspects of your life and define a focus for each area.

Personal/Emotional

This is where you think about your development as a human being. This includes things like: reading, writing and time alone to think. If the personal/emotional aspect of your life is out of whack, so is everything else.

Alone time is important for a number of reasons. First, it's difficult to ever have a real sense of who you are as a person if you're never alone to think about it. And if you're always surrounded by other people, deep self-examination is impossible.

Alone time is also important because it's in the quiet moments that great ideas tend to spring forth. You will rarely be struck by a great way to solve a problem in a room full of people.

More often than not, great moments of genius come to us when we are quiet and alone. Give yourself time to find your inner genius.

Business/Work
Ask yourself these questions:
- Am I happy doing what I'm doing?
- Do I feel like I'm making a difference?
- What am I trying to achieve at work?
- Do I have a career or a job? Which do I want?
- Am I chiefly concerned with making money, or is getting a sense of fulfillment from what I do, my number one priority?

Answer these questions and you'll find what parts of your work life are going well and what needs work. Next, define a focus based on those needs.

Relationships
Of course the first of these is your marriage or romantic relationship. You should also include your relationships with family and friends. Without a few key personal relationships which we can depend on, the world is a lonely place.

In other chapters I discussed that relationships require nurturing. If you nurture one relationship at the expense of all the others, you have problems. Focus on what you want from your relationships, what others expect of you and work on meeting those expectations. Let everything else go.

Physical

Your health is of critical importance (whether you treat it that way or not) so it belongs in its own category. Manage good nutrition and find time for exercise, sleep and relaxation. These are important parts of your physical life.

The idea isn't to focus on weight loss. Focus on overall health. There are heavy people who are sick and heavy people who are healthy.

Work to make sure that you eat well, get enough sleep and exercise every day. If one of these elements is lacking that's where you should focus.

Spiritual

Your relationship with your God is important. I've been guilty of letting this aspect of my life slip find more time for the others and I've suffered for it every time. Don't make the same mistake.

When I was waiting for my transplant, I prayed often. Some - times, several times a day. And while quantity is important, quality is more critical.

Spirituality isn't a luxury, it's a necessity. Someone once said, "We are all spiritual beings on a human journey". Don't forget your spiritual side.

Community

This includes your interactions with the world around you: volunteer work, financial contributions, staying on top of current events. Your life does not happen in a vacuum. It's important to be a part of the whole, not simply existing as an individual.

These headings are the ones I have drafted for my own life. They are not written in stone. You may have different interpretations or categories for your life and that's okay. The point is simply that you categorize your life in order to better understand your priorities.

In Black & White

The next step is to find a priority or goal for each aspect of your life that you listed. I encourage you to put a time limit on that goal. A goal without a time limit isn't a goal. But we talk about that later. Time limits also force us to address these priorities more often.

What's great about taking the time to write down these objectives is that often it's a journey of self-discovery. It can help you to focus on what you really want in your life, something many of us struggle to figure out.

Now for the real challenge, after you've articulated a singular focus for each aspect of your life, you have to stick to it! As a result of the busy world we live in, most of us have become multi-taskers either by design or by accident and so it can be very difficult to remain focused on any one thing for very long, but I encourage you to try. By focusing on one thing and clearing away everything else, you'll be able to make much quicker progress.

"Time is the coin of your life. It is the only coin you have, and only you can determine how it will be spent. Be careful lest you let other people spend it for you." – Carl Sandburg

CHAPTER 42

Make Time for What Counts to You

When was the last time you took an inventory of your priorities? What is number one on your list? I consider this a powerful and important question, important enough that I ask it of myself often.

I ask this question a lot as a way of ensuring that my actions are in line with my priorities. Stephen Covey, author of *The Seven Habits of Highly Successful People*, calls this congruence.

To live in total congruence is a personal goal. It means living in such a way that our ideas, motives and actions are perfectly aligned. Ideally it means that ideally that if you said your family is your number one priority, you spend more hours with your family than anything else.

You're probably thinking, "I can't possibly spend more time with my family than I do at work. If I did, I couldn't pay the bills. There aren't enough hours in the day and there aren't jobs out there where you can work twenty hours a week." True. But, if your work is to support your family that counts as family time as long as you work to support your family and not to avoid them.

Do a thorough check of your priorities, and see how congruently you're living. For example, if physical health is your second or third priority but you're 25, 30 or even 50 lbs overweight and can't remember the last time you exercised, you need to re-evaluate your priorities, your actions, or both.

THERE IS HAPPINESS TO BE FOUND WHEN YOUR CALENDAR MATCHES YOUR PRIORITIES

If you rank your spiritual life as your main priority but routinely skip church to sleep in or watch the big football game, you're not living in congruence.

If personal development is a priority I ask you what was the last book you read or CD you listened to? When was the last time you took 30 minutes alone to think?

Where is watching TV on your priority list? If it is low, but you spend more than 20 hrs per week in front of the tube (Stats Canada says we average of about 25 hours a week watching TV) you're not living in congruence.

Living in congruence isn't easy. I'm not sure how many ever really get all the way there. But, as with many valuable things in life, the pursuit is as important as the destination.

Living in congruence is important because failure can wreak havoc on your emotional, psychological and even physical life. When we don't live congruently we begin to feel a sense of inner turmoil, as though one part of us is fighting against another.

The more congruently you live, the better your calendar matches your priorities and the more what you say matches what you do, the happier, more successful and more content you'll be. If your life isn't as congruent as it should be, start doing something about it today.

In Black & White

If you feel like you're living congruently now, congratulations. You're doing what many aren't able to do. If you feel like you have work to do in this area, keep reading, I have a few suggestions that may help.

This week make a concerted effort to spend more time on your number one priority. If your life is totally incongruent right now, you won't turn that around instantly. It may take months or years to get things where you want them to be. But you'll never get there if you don't start somewhere.

Start by evaluating each area of your life and prioritize them: Family, Spiritual, Physical, Career and Personal. Where does each aspect of life rank on your priority list?

My Top Priorities:

1. _____

2. _____

3. _____

Look at your calendar. Do a tally of how many hours you spent on each aspect of your life. How does it compare to your priority list? Are your calendar and priority list in sync?

Take action today to get your life into better alignment. It's work and requires discipline, but it yields great rewards. Happiness is found when your calendar matches your priorities.

What I Spent the Most Time on Last Month:

1. _____

2. _____

3. _____

"What's money? A man is a success if he gets up in the morning and goes to bed at night and in between does what he wants to do."– **Bob Dylan**

CHAPTER 43

Beware the Lure of Money

No amount of money is worth trading your happiness for. It's not that I believe money is bad. I think money is a great thing. I enjoy having it and spending it. But no amount of money is worth trading your happiness for. So before you pursue a career or an opportunity because of the financial rewards it offers, take a minute to consider the consequences.

Contrary to what some believe, money can be dangerous. It can ruin lives and I'm not talking about drugs, alcohol, or gambling. The problems I refer to are more subtle but just as tragic. I refer to the thousands, even millions of people, who waste their lives away working in a job they hate simply because it "pays well".

How many people to do you know who work in a job they hate? I'll bet you know a few people who let money decide their career. You might be one of them.

Lying in a hospital bed, facing my death, I promised myself that if I ever got out of the hospital I would live life fully. I wouldn't waste time working at a job that I didn't enjoy no matter how much money I was offered.

After I recovered from my transplant I was faced with the hard reality that if I ever wanted to move out on my own, I had to find a job. At 24 I didn't want live with my parents any longer. After attempting to find something fun and exciting in my field of interest, I settled for a job at an insurance company.

It was a good job, it paid okay and the work wasn't too stressful. The only problem was I hated it. I spent days sitting behind a desk when my personality is better suited to working with people. I spent my days doing repetitive tasks that required attention to detail and no creativity. It was totally contrary to my skill set.

I soon realized that if I was going to feel fulfilled, I had to find another career. That's when I discovered motivational speaking.

Following my dream of being a speaker meant taking a big risk. I had to leave a steady job with a regular salary, start from scratch without clients, and had no one to tell me what to do next. It was exciting. But it was also very scary. I encourage you to do something you love. But I don't suggest that you pursue your dreams at the expense of everything else.

The first three years of my speaking career I was part-time work. To make it work for our family, I needed another job so we could pay the bills. But I still made time for my passion and it's paying off now.

MONEY AND SECURITY AREN'T WORTH MUCH IF YOU'RE WEALTHY, SECURE, AND *MISERABLE*

Countless people have given up big dreams and goals in exchange for money and security. How sad. What these people inevitably discover is that money and security aren't worth much if you're wealthy, secure and *miserable*.

If you aren't happy with what you're doing now, if you dread going to work, then think about what it is that you'd really like to do and start working on a plan. Plan how you can make the jump from where you are to where you want to be. Remember not to jump in blind. Plan how you'll support yourself and your family. But you will have to *jump* at some point.

Making a career change and pursuing your passion takes courage. Risk is involved but don't let that scare you. The reward is worth it. After all; can you put a value on waking up excited to go to work every day?

Don't let your dreams and goals slip away from you for a few steady bucks. Don't wake up one day 30 years from now and realize that your bank balance is in good shape but your emotional and life-satisfaction accounts are overdrawn. No amount of money is worth that.

In Black & White

If you feel like money has driven you and your decisions, money might be more important to you than it should be. I suggest you take this challenging test:
Take a week off from money.

Spend a week without spending any more than absolutely necessary. You need to fill your gas tank and put food in the fridge, but you don't *need* that latte in the morning and you don't need to buy your lunch when you can brown bag it.

A week off spending will do a few things for you. First, by taking a week off from money you discover where you spending it. People spend unconsciously and wonder where money went at the end of the month. Take a week off from money and see where it goes.

The benefit of this exercise is that it will help you realize that you're not as dependent on money as you thought. You'll see that with a few sacrifices, you can get along with a whole lot less. More importantly, you'll realize that life is about the experiences you have and the people you share them with, not the things you own or the money you have.

"Family is a life jacket in the stormy sea of life."
– J.K. Rowling

CHAPTER 44

Talk to Your Family

Family is a universal element of the human experience. Our experience of what it means to have a family isn't universal. But no matter who you are, where you come from, or what you do, you have or had a family.

In this chapter I want to help you consider what your family means to you and whether or not you're giving these important people the time and love they deserve.

Let me say up front that I'm fortunate to have an incredible family. They're supportive, loving, kind and I love them very much. While they may occasionally drive me nuts (find me a family that doesn't drive each other a little crazy sometimes) I can't imagine my life without them.

I'm writing with an acknowledged bias. I think family is important and I believe family is one of life's greatest blessings. If your family experience hasn't been as positive as mine, there's a good chance you may not feel the same way. That's okay.

I hope that by reading this chapter, you find it easier to see the good things about your family and appreciate whatever form of family you have in your life.

I come from a family of six; three younger brothers, myself, my Mom and my Dad. I'm one of the lucky ones among my generation. My parents stayed together and still love each other after thirty years of marriage. I love my parents very much. But what's special is that they are the kind of people I admire. They're such amazing people. I'd love them even if they weren't my parents. They have big hearts, they genuinely care about others and they do their best to make the world around them a better place.

My brothers Neil, Greg, and Scott (ages 20, 17 and 15 at the time of my transplant) were amazing too. They were always good brothers but when I got sick they were incredibly selfless and mature. Having one of my parents with me all the time meant that they *missed* one of their parents for most of that a year. In some cases Mom and Dad were both with me and they took care of themselves, not an easy task for teenagers. But they did it and without complaint.

I'm ashamed to say that I haven't always appreciated them as I should. After I graduated high school and went off to university I was grateful to be out on my own. I loved the independence, the ability to make my own decisions and the fact that I didn't have to share things with my brothers anymore.

For a long time I took the relationship I had with my family for granted. I mistakenly thought that I didn't need them any more. I went home some weekends and holidays and I enjoyed being home. But when I didn't get home for a few weeks or months, it wasn't a big deal. I was grown-up now, self-sufficient. Then I got sick.

LIFE IS TOO SHORT NOT TO TAKE EVERY OPPORTUNITY TO APPRECIATE THE SPECIAL PEOPLE IN YOUR LIFE

When I was put on the transplant waiting list I was told that I needed to have a support person with me at all times. Either my Mom or Dad had to move to Toronto with me to wait for the surgery to be put on the list. I remember thinking that this was a silly rule. After all, I was 22 years old. I'd be fine. Why did I need my Mommy or Daddy with me?

After a few months on the list it became clear why I needed support. The waiting and the worrying took an emotional and physical toll. Many times I felt frustrated and scared. There were times when, at twenty-three, I could be found crying in my mothers arms.

Time was running out. Worrying about what would happen to me next was all I could think about. If it weren't for my parents being there to distract me, comfort me and make me laugh, I don't know if I'd be here today.

Before the surgery I wrote a letter to each member of my family. In the letters I wrote for pages about what each of them meant to me and how much I loved them. Looking back, I wonder why I took the threat of imminent death to make it okay to share my feelings? I encourage you not to make the same mistake.

In Black and White

My illness taught me that life is too short to miss opportunities to appreciate the special people in your life.

If you have a wonderful relationship and love your family members, take time to make sure they know how you feel. If your relationship with your family isn't as strong as it should be, start working to fix it. Someday it will be too late to say "I'm sorry" or "I love you" to the people who need to hear that from you.

Take time this week to make phone calls or pay a few visits to your family. Let them know how much you care about them. It will mean a lot to them (whether they acknowledge it or not) and it will make you feel good too.

"A man should keep his friendships in constant repair."
–Samuel Johnson

CHAPTER 45

Keep in Touch

When was the last time you spoke to your best friend or your college roommate?

Depending on your personality, lifestyle, and even your gender you answer the questions differently. You may differ about how long is too long not to speak to someone you care about.

Life is too short to neglect good friends. You never know when your last chance will come to say "I love you", or "You really mean a lot to me". September 11th taught many people that lesson the hard way. Take advantage of every chance you get to connect with those who matter most.

After waiting a year for a miracle to save my life and unsure if I would see many of my friends again, there were many things I wanted to change about the way I lived my life. One of the most important was that I stay in touch with my friends and family.

Friendships and family are precious, but often underappreciated, gifts. Think about it, your family loves you and cares for you better than anyone else in the world. They've known you longer than anyone and you can always count on them no matter what.

YOU NEVER KNOW WHEN THE LAST CHANCE WILL COME TO SAY, "I LOVE YOU" OR "I REALLY CARE ABOUT YOU"

Your friends know you well too. They're great for laughing when you're up and comforting you when you're down. They're your refuge from the storms of life. They're the first ones that you share your joys and sorrows with. You can tell them anything and know that they'll love you unconditionally.

Unfortunately, when things get stressful, and time is at a premium, it's our families and friends that suffer. They bear the brunt of our frustrations and are ignored when there aren't enough hours in the day. Maybe it's because we know that they'll be there no matter what, that we feel that it's acceptable to ignore and mistreat them. Friends and family relationships, no matter how strong, still need periodic maintenance. In order to thrive they need nurture and care like any other living thing.

It's been a year since my grandfather died. My grandfather was a great man, and he was a great man, a great grandfather and was better than anyone I know at nurturing the relationships in his life. I don't think I've known anyone who had more friends. His funeral service was packed and I know it was because of how well he nurtured relationships.

My grandfather had an address book. Like many address books, it had names, addresses and phone numbers of his friends and family members in it. But it also had birthdates, anniversary dates, children's and grandchildren's names and birthdays and any other information that was important to that person. What was truly unique about that book wasn't what was in it, but how often it was used.

My grandfather was great at doing what many of us fail to do; he called every person in that book regularly. He called on birthdays, which he never forgot, and other special occasions; he also called for no real reason at all. As he got older and dementia began to take its toll, he often called people a great distance away at all hours of the day and night just to say "hi". That was his nature.

My grandfather was always a very busy person. He worked for more than 30 years as a salesman in the days before email and faxes and electronic ordering. He was on the road all of the time and had little spare time, but that didn't stop him from making time for the things that really mattered to him, his friends and family.

He really cared about his friends, as we all do, but what he did better than anyone I've ever known, is he made sure that his friends *knew* how much he cared about them. People appreciated that. It made them want to be his friend. It made them feel special. How great would it be if you could do that for your friends?

In Black & White

This week contact three people you haven't spoken to in at least a month. It might have been a whole lot longer than a month and that's okay. The point is we tend to speak to the same small group frequently but we neglect others whom we also care for.

There are a few stipulations to how you make these contacts. If you're going to make the effort to contact someone that you haven't spoken to in a while, make sure you have the time to do it properly.

1. Make sure that when you talk with this person, on the phone or face to face, that you leave enough time to do it properly. (An hour seems like a good time frame.) You can't make a meaningful reconnection in ten minutes.
2. Make the conversation meaningful. You don't have to impose artificial structure to your conversation, but try to ask insightful questions and share meaningful parts of your life. Avoid exchanging superficial pleasantries and talking about the weather! You haven't seen this person in a while you should have lots to talk about.
3. Last but not least do it now! Don't put this off. Resist the temptation to say that you're too busy or you don't really feel like it today. There will always be other things that you do. That's how a few days become a week and then a month.

Pretty soon it's been a year since you've spoken with some of the people you care a great deal about.

Make today the day you make the first phone call. It'll be fun, and your friend will appreciate it, I promise.

*"Too many people don't care what happens as long as it
doesn't happen to them."*
– Anonymous

CHAPTER 46

Don't Let Apathy Take Over

When was the last time that you went to the grocery store, airport, video store, bank and the person working behind the counter failed to say, "Hello" and "thank you"? Sadly, I bet it wasn't long ago.

I'm only twenty-nine. In the last ten years I've noticed an erosion of politeness. Surely, readers who remember the 50s and 60s will notice greater changes.

Is it a coincidence that our world seems more violent and the gap between the rich and the poor grows at a time where simple courtesies have become too much for to bother with? I don't think so. Our electronic world has let us forget how to connect or extend the simple courtesies to each other.

In a world of emails and instant messaging, simply talking to each other is rare. While the world is "smaller" due to our ability to communicate with anyone in the world, this has made us less effective at communicating with those we are close to.

Call me crazy, but I think that our failure to communicate well is related to the 50%+ divorce rate or the disparity between rich and poor. If we all felt more connected to each other, cared more about each other, I truly believe these problems would improve. So what can you do?

IN A WORLD WITH TOO MUCH WAR, CRIME AND HUNGER, WE NEED MORE OF THE LITTLE THINGS THAT LET US KNOW THAT SOMEONE CARES.

What you shouldn't do is allow the problem to overwhelm you so that you do nothing. Divide and conquer instead. If lots of people do little things we can turn things around.

In a world with war, crime and hunger, we need more little things that let us know we matter and that someone cares; things like hugs, smiles and laughter. These things are so lacking that earlier this year Juan Mann stood on a corner in Chicago with a sign advertising that he was giving away free hugs. He created such a stir than he landed on Oprah!

The idea that someone would be kind to total strangers is so foreign that it's a novelty.

One day a few years ago, I decided I would try to do a random act of kindness for someone. I was in line at the grocery store and the lady in front of me had only two items so I offered to pay for her order just to be nice. I told the lady at the register that she could add the other lady's order to mine.

What was the lady's reaction? She freaked! She became defensive and frightened, as if I must have an ulterior motive for being nice. Rather than being appreciative, she was suspicious, and would not allow me to pay the two or three dollars on her behalf.

At first when I retold that story to friends and family I laughed. I thought the lady's reaction was pretty funny. But as time passed, I realized her reaction was actually sad. This poor woman was so jaded, that the idea that a stranger would do something nice for her, "just because" was incomprehensible. How sad.

In Black & White

There are dozens of things that we can do everyday to make a difference in the world. Some are large, some small. Following are a few suggestions for what you can do to make the world a little better for someone else:

Hug someone – I recommend someone you know but whatever works for you.

Smile at a stranger – Smile at people as you walk down the street. Some people will think you're weird but I'd rather be weird than apathetic.

Mow a Lawn or Shovel a Driveway – The next time you're out doing chores, do your neighbour's work too. They're sure to be appreciative and the small gesture will likely strengthen your relationship.

Hold a Door – It takes five seconds, but people appreciate it.

Imagine how different our world would be if we all did just a few of these simple, yet powerful, things every day?

Holding a door won't solve the world's problems but it won't hurt either. It's often said that if you're not part of the solution, you're part of the problem. What are you doing to be part of the solution?

"The name of the game is taking care of yourself, because you're going to live long enough to wish that you had."
– **Grace Mirabella**

CHAPTER 47

Take Care of # 1

If this chapter seems to contradict what I've already written about giving to others, allow me to explain. This book is about living life, real life, and real life is full of dualities. Those whom we love the most are also those who can hurt us the most. The biggest obstacles in life can also be great opportunities. Giving to others, while taking care of ourselves, is another one of the dualities in life.

So if you read the title of this chapter and hear me say that you should be selfish, you're right. It's okay to be selfish sometimes. But that does not mean it isn't important to give to others. You need to do both.

Let me suggest that this chapter may speak more to women than to men, although us guys can probably learn a few things here too. Ladies; before you write letters, allow me to explain.

The reason that women may learn more from this chapter than men is because women are more likely to be self*less*. They may forget to take care of themselves. As wives and mothers, women often fall into the trap of continually giving without taking any time for themselves. The problem with that is when you live that way long enough, you may wake up to discover that you have nothing left to give.

YOU'VE BEEN GIVEN LIFE,
YOUR RESPONSIBILITY IS
TO PROTECT
IT AND USE IT
AS EFFECTIVELY
AS POSSIBLE

Taking care of each other is a fundamental part of our humanity. But you can't take care of someone else without taking care of yourself first. You can't give what you don't have. If you tend to give too much try these suggestions for taking better care of yourself.

In Black & White

Start taking better care of your most important asset, you.

Get your rest: Do you remember the last time that you slept for eight hours in a row? If not, get to bed earlier. Remember, getting to bed early counts. Science has proven that the quality of rest is determined not only by how many hours of sleep you get but *when* you get them.

Eat right – Fruit flavored candy doesn't count as a serving of fruit. Coffee with milk doesn't count as breakfast. In our busy lives, it is tough finding time to make balanced meals. But a little planning and preparation will ensure that you get balanced nutrition.

Exercise – If getting up to change the channel when you can't find the remote seems like an incredible hardship, you're not sweating enough.

Try to get 20-30 minutes of vigorous activity three times a week. That small investment of time can make a huge difference in your health, energy level and mood.

Take Time to Get Your Life in Order – You can't effectively support a friend through a break up, or help your mate with problems at work, if your life is secretly in shambles.

Be strong enough to admit when you need help.

Taking care of you is not selfish, it's smart. It's your responsibility to your family and yourself. You've been given life. Your responsibility is to protect it and use it as effectively as possible.

"If you knew what I know about the power of giving,
you would not let a single meal pass without sharing
it in some way." – **Buddha**

CHAPTER 48

Give as Much and as Often as You Can

"They're lazy." They should just go get a job!" "They probably make more money than I do." "Half of them are kids from the suburbs looking to make an easy buck!" These are some of the reasons I was given for why I shouldn't give money to panhandlers or homeless people on the street, but I do it all the time anyway.

Let me say right away that I don't tell you that so you'll think I'm a hero to these people. I know I'm not saving their lives by giving them a little change. At the most, I give a couple of dollars. I'm not changing their lives with that money, but I still give it and if I could, I would give more.

Why? Because I believe that the "reasons" for not helping someone in need aren't reasons; they're excuses. I believe it's our responsibility to take every opportunity we can to help make the lives of those around us better.

Now you may think that guys like me who give money on the street are suckers. In some situations you're probably right. I'm sure there are times when I've been taken advantage of by someone who doesn't need the money, or someone who's going to spend it on booze or drugs instead of food or shelter. But there are always people who abuse the generosity of others. People abuse Medicare and Worker's Compensation too. Does that mean we should eliminate those things for everyone because some people are going to take advantage of it? I don't think so.

❦

IT'S OUR RESPONSIBILITY TO TAKE ADVANTAGE OF EVERY OPPORTUNITY TO MAKE THE LIVES OF THOSE AROUND US BETTER

There will always be people who take advantage. I'm sure I've been hustled into giving money to someone who doesn't really need it. But I decided a long time ago that I'd rather give to fifty people who didn't need it, than not give to one person who did.

I wonder why it is that so many otherwise kind and generous people are unwilling to help those who are most in need. How is it that we can spend $5 on a cup of coffee but shudder at the thought of throwing a dollar in a cup to help a fellow human being who slept on the street last night?

How can normally sympathetic and compassionate people walk by the homeless and destitute and not give them a second thought? It's not because we're heartless or don't care. I think it's because we're so detached from one another that our sphere of consciousness has shrunk to the point that many live in our own little world.

For all of the developments in communication technology our world has become a lonelier place. In many ways we're increasingly disconnected from each other. As a result, we seem to be increasingly less affected by the trials of our fellow human beings. Even today with all of the resources we have and technological advances we have made, people are still starving, and wars are killing innocent victims and forcing even more to flee their homes. Yet many of us are content to live in ignorance while our fellow human beings suffer inhumane conditions.

Can you stop these atrocities by giving change to a kid on the street? Of course not. But generosity is the key to making the world a better place. As the old saying goes, generosity begins at home.

When you act out of generosity, you have to open your heart. When that happens, and only when that happens, we can begin to affect change in the lives of others and in the world. If we all opened our hearts to others' struggles the world would be a better place.

In Black & White

Someone once said, "Man was created for other men".

This week find five things that you can do for someone else. Do you have to give away thousands of dollars? No. Money is fine, but there a lots of ways to make a difference are 100% FREE.

A woman in our community had the idea of sending valentines to men and women serving in our military in Afghanistan. She started a city-wide campaign with the goal of sending at least one valentine to every soldier from our area.

Community members, including those from neighbouring towns and cities, pitched in. School kids created home-made valentines. By the end of the two-week campaign, she collected more than 50,000 cards that were then sent to the local military base and then shipped to Afghanistan in time for Valentine's Day.

Did that lady stop the war? No. Did she single-handedly change the world? No. Did she take action and affect change that could multiply and spread to touch thousands of other people? Absolutely.

Hold a door for someone. Help an elderly person with their yard work or their groceries. Visit a friend or relative who might be feeling lonely. Take the new guy at work or school out to lunch. Give something to someone else. When you do, an amazing thing happens; you'll help two people feel a little better about life and the world around them. You and them.

How can I give something this week to make the world around me a little better?

*"Live is an echo. What you send out – comes back. What you reap –
you sow. What you give – you get"* – Unknown

CHAPTER 49

The Give/Get
Multiplication Principal

Have you ever heard the saying "What you give is what you get?" Maybe you've heard, "what goes around comes around" or maybe you've heard it referred to as "karma". Do you believe it? I used to, but I don't anymore. That's why I made this amend - ment to it. I believe that you don't get what you give; you get what you give many, many times over.

Have you ever seen a commercial for a charity that helps needy children in Africa? You know the ones that show starving, ill, needy children who have virtually nothing and they ask you for a few cents a day to help feed and care for them? We've all seen these commercials. Sometimes we change the channel, sometimes we don't. How many times have you called the number and actually done something?

I often wonder why we don't give more than we do. Many people are very generous but almost all of us could be giving more than we do. Why don't we?

For a long time I couldn't make sense of this contradiction. Then I heard the reason vocalized in a single word: scarcity. I don't know whose theory it was originally, but scarcity or a false belief in scarcity is what prevents us from being as generous as we should, be.

What is scarcity?

The theory of scarcity says that to give something to you I have to lose something; what I give to you, I don't have anymore. It works on the idea that the world is a finite place. Scarcity theory says that there is a limited quantity of everything and so the more of something I give the less I have for myself.

The truth is that for many things in life, important things, the scarcity theory doesn't apply. Love, caring, empathy and energy are all limitless. You can give away as much as you want and you won't have less. In fact, you'll have more.

YOU DON'T GET WHAT YOU GIVE, YOU GET WHAT YOU GIVE MULTIPLIED MANY TIMES OVER

I believe that it's virtually impossible to give anything to someone else without simultaneously helping yourself. Often you gain more than the recipient of your gift. The world is an incredibly limitless place that will not only pay you back whatever kindnesses you offer, but will multiply them several times over and send them back to you. Let me explain...

In order to become more generous, a goal I think we all should have, we must learn that scarcity is not an issue with things like caring, compassion and love. There may be a limit to the gold in a mine or oil in a field, but is there a limit to the love a mother has for her child? Is there a limit to the care grandfather gives to his grandson? Of course not. Why? Because things like love and compassion don't decrease when given, they multiply.

In Black & White

Everyday we are given opportunities to give. We have to decide if we'll take advantage of those opportunities?

If you are looking for good reasons to give and asking yourself, "What's in it for me? What do I get out of giving?" you may be missing the point. Here are two answers:

1) It makes you feel great – Few things that will ever make you feel as fulfilled and satisfied as giving.

2) Giving always comes back – It may not be immediately obvious, but somewhere, somehow, giving something to someone else will benefit you.

Take time this week to find a way that you can give something to someone else.

"Never doubt that a small group of dedicated citizens can change the world. It's the only thing that ever has."
– **Margaret Meade**

CHAPTER 50

Make an Impact

When a rock hits a pond it causes ripples that reach far beyond the point of impact. I believe that life gives us two basic options: we can either take action and make an impact on the world or we can do nothing and be impacted by the world. What choice will you make?

Your life is busy. It's not uncommon to feel like you're living from one task, duty or event to the next with little time for thought and reflection.

Before long you're so bogged down managing your day to day life that you're not at the helm of your ship anymore. The current, not you, is determining where you're going.

Don't allow that to happen unless you're content to have your life ruled by circumstances. (If you were content to do that you probably wouldn't read this book.)

Don't let life rule you, rule your life. One of my life goals is to use my life to make an impact on the world. Do I think that I can single handedly change the world? No. Few people can do that. But I DO believe that I can make a positive impact.

LIVE GIVES YOU A CHOICE, YOU CAN TAKE ACTION AND IMPACT THE WORLD, OR YOU CAN DO NOTHING AND LET THE WORLD IMPACT YOU

Think of people like Bono, Oprah, and Gandhi. I would argue that they have changed the world. Some would agree, others might not, but there is no arguing that they have made an impact. The world is different today than it would be if they hadn't been in it.

You may disagree. You're thinking, 'Hey Mark isn't there still violence, still poverty, still hatred?" Sure. So have these people really changed anything? Absolutely! While there are still lots of things wrong with the world, there are also millions of lives around the world that will never be the same after having been touched, helped, influenced and inspired by the work of these incredible people.

So what's stopping you from making the same kind of impact?

In Black & White

What is the difference between Bono, Oprah, and Gandhi and the rest of us? Other than the fact that everyone knows their names, they take action. These people aren't ones to sit idle. They don't just talk about what's wrong with the world. They identify issues and then they DO something about it.

So what are you doing? What action have you taken to solve the problems you're passionate about?

There isn't enough time and you don't have enough energy to solve ALL of the world's problems. So pick an issue that you're passionate about. This week research the issue and come up with some actions that you can take to make a difference. Great things are accomplished by "ordinary" people all the time. That's what makes ordinary people extraordinary.

"Don't worry if your job is small,
And your rewards are few;
Remember that the mighty oak
Was once a nut like you. "
— Anonymous

CHAPTER 51
Great Things Happen
A Little at a Time

I wrote earlier about "the Power of Beginning". Starting is often the hardest part of the process of achieving our goals. But it doesn't mean that the rest of the journey will be easy. To stay motivated to achieve your dreams remember this important lesson: great things happen a little at a time.

It is rare if not impossible to find something of value that can be achieved instantly. Think about it. Reflect on the best moments of your life: graduation, getting married, the birth of a child, or landing a big job. I'll bet that not one of those things happened instantly.

THE KEY TO SUCCEEDING AT ANYTHING IN LIFE IS TO FOCUS ON THE SMALL VICTORIES

Realizing those goals may happen in a moment or a day. But it takes weeks, months, even years for some goals to progress from idea to achievement. Graduation is one of the great achievements in a person's life; it takes at least four years. Landing the perfect job can take years and even decades in some cases. While a wedding takes a few minutes, cultivating a relationship that will last takes much more time.

If we know that goals take time to achieve, why do we often give up on goals not long after starting? I think a big reason is that when progress slows we are easily discouraged. When things are moving forward, it's okay. But when progress slows doubt starts to take over and we wonder if we'll ever get there. Have you ever felt that way?

The key to succeeding at anything in life is to focus on small goals so that you get a sense of progress until you reach the big goal.

Remember when you were little and your parents took you on a trip? Remember what it was like to be fifteen and waiting the last few months to turn sixteen and get your driver's license? Sometimes it feels as if we'll never reach our goal. But if you can stay focused and keep moving forward, eventually you'll get there.

Running hills is part of my marathon training. It's really tough. But I know it will help me reach my goal of running faster. When I'm struggling to get up a hill I often break the goal down into smaller steps. I set a goal to run to the next telephone pole. Then I run to the one after that.

When your goals seem a long way off, and your motivation wanes, remember that great things happen a little at a time and run to the next pole.

In Black & White

When striving to attain a goal, create a "picture" of what you want. I put the word "picture" in quotation marks because it doesn't have to be a literal picture. In some cases a picture works well. The point is to create a vision of where you want to go so that you have something to keep you focused and motivated throughout the process.

For example; if you're trying to lose weight, cut out a picture of a fit person and paste it somewhere where you'll see it often. If it's a career goal, create a vision of the position and lifestyle that you want to attain.

By creating a clear picture of what you want, you'll be able to stay focused and avoid the distractions that can prevent you from reaching your goals.

*"Consider the postage stamp: its usefulness consists in the
ability to stick to one thing until it gets there "*
– Otto Van Bismarck

CHAPTER 52

Refuse to Quit

As a marathon runner, this concept is invaluable to me. There
is no way that I would ever finish a 42.2 km run without
making the decision before I start, that barring a horrific injury,
I will finish no matter what.

When I ran my first marathon, I reached the 32km mark, the
race is 42.2km, and was pretty sure I didn't have anything left.
I couldn't run anymore. The tank was empty. I started to walk.

I slowed down to the point that I was almost standing still. I
seriously thought about quitting. Then it hit me. I had to look
at my hand. Let me explain…

On my hand I'd written the names of three people I met while
waiting for a transplant who died before they could get new
organs. I realized that I could have been one of them but I wasn't.

Not only was I alive, I was healthy. I was healthy enough to be
running a marathon. My health was a gift I'd been given and
my job was to use it.

When I realized that I knew I *had* to give a little bit more. Yes I
was tired. Yes I wanted to stop but I couldn't. I had to find a
way to give just a little bit more.

Slowly I put one foot in front of the other. I repeated that
motion over and over again. I realized that as long as I could
keep putting one foot in front of the other, I would eventually
reach the finish line. So that's what I did. I dug deep. I found
energy that I didn't think was there and I finished the race.
That's what I challenge you to do.

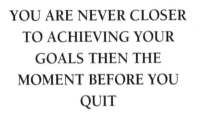

YOU ARE NEVER CLOSER TO ACHIEVING YOUR GOALS THEN THE MOMENT BEFORE YOU QUIT

In each of my presentations I shock people by saying that I
firmly believe no one in the history of the world has ever failed
at anything. That may sound bold or trite depending on how
you receive it. But I still believe that it's true. The truth is;
failing doesn't make you a failure, failing to try again when you
fail makes you a failure. You are never closer to achieving your
goals then the moment right before you quit.

So decide today that you aren't going to give up on your
dreams until you achieve them. You may not succeed the first
time. It may take dozens of attempts to reach your goal. But as
long as you continue to strive for what you want, as long as
you refuse to give up, merely in the attempt you will have
succeeded.

In Black and White

Make a commitment today that you will not stop working on your goals until you reach them.

The following is an oath that I get attendees at my presentations to take. It's a promise to yourself to take your goals seriously. I encourage you to photocopy it and post it somewhere where you'll see it often. Take it seriously. If you only keep one promise in your life, keep this one to yourself.

The Oath

I (your name here) hereby promise to take this card and put it somewhere where I will see it everyday.

I promise not to let my self-doubt take over, believe others when they say I can't do it or put off my dreams. Life is too short for that.

I promise to look at this, my dream, everyday and let it serve as a reminder of what I KNOW I am capable of. And when I have doubts, I promise to remember that ANYTHING is POSSIBLE.

If you only remember one thing you've read in this entire book, please remember this. No matter how hard things get, now matter how hopeless things may seem, never, ever, EVER, GIVE UP! If you never give up, you will never fail!

About the author

Mark Black is the founder of Mark Black Speaks, a speaking and coaching firm that helps people awaken their hidden greatness. Mark has spoken to thousands of people from coast to coast, including events for corporations, associations, conference and educational institutions. To learn more about what Mark can do for your company, organization or school go to his website:

www.MarkBlack.ca

Presentations

Mark is available to speak to corporations, associations and educa tional institutions throughout the year. Mark's powerful presentations have received rave reviews from people across the country and are ideal for opening and closing conferences or as training sessions for professional development days. Information about all of Mark's presentations are available on the website.

Newsletter & Articles

Mark produces a weekly motivation article entitled "Mark's Motivational Minute? that provides ideas to help you to stay motivated to achieve your goals. A FREE subscription and archives of past articles are available on his website.

Coaching

Mark offers personal life/achievement coaching to help people awaken their greatness and realize their potential. If you are interested in having Mark as your personal life coach, go to his Coaching page on his website or email Mark@MarkBlack.ca and put "coaching" in the subject line.

CPSIA information can be obtained
at www.ICGtesting.com
Printed in the USA
JSHW022117041122
32619JS00002B/15